THE NEW
BERNESE
MOUNTAIN DOG

Sharon Chesnutt Smith

HOWELL
BOOK HOUSE
New York

HOWELL BOOK HOUSE
Macmillan General Reference
A Simon & Schuster Macmillan Company
1633 Broadway
New York, NY 10019-6785

Library of Congress Cataloging-in-Publication Data
Smith, Sharon Chesnutt.
    The new Bernese mountain dog / Sharon Chesnutt Smith.
        p.   cm.
    ISBN 0-87605-075-5
    1. Bernese mountain dog.   I. Title.
SF429.B47S58   1994
636.7'3—dc20   94-16804
                                                     CIP

Manufactured in the United States of America

10 9 8 7 6 5

Dedicated to the two great influences in my life that I lost while working on this book.

First, to my beloved father,
James Horace Chesnutt (1924–1994).
He taught me that hard work is its own reward, and to never start something unless you intend to finish it. Without his influence I would have given up on the sport of dogs many times in the face of the many disasters Mother Nature loves to bestow on dog breeders.

Secondly, to my Bernese Mountain Dog
Ch. Arthos October v. Berndash (1984–1994).
He introduced me to this breed as no other could—Best in Show, Top Conformation Dog, and Top Producer. His qualities in temperament and movement set the standard for me to breed by.

Not a day goes by that I do not think of them both.

DINNER WITH A BERNESE

"Dinner with a Bernese" by Ron Young is a popular cartoon among Bernese fans who happily share their lives with the breed in spite of the mayhem the breed's innate friendliness may bring about. Bear in mind that humor is based, in part, on exaggeration, so consider the cartoon accordingly and enjoy!

Contents

Am., Can. Ch. Gitana De Braye, Am., Can. CD (Can. Ch. Xodi v. Grunenmatt, Can. CDX, Am. CD, ex Ericka De Braye), owned by Eve Menegoz and bred by Willy Fawer, mirrors the handsome sturdiness of this stalwart Swiss working dog.

Paw Prints, Inc.

Am., Can. Ch. Big Paws Baron, a Best in Show winner owned by Gina McDonnell, models the "Berner's" typical, kindly head and expression.

Foreword

THE BOOK you now have in your hand represents a significant milestone in the history of its subject, the Bernese Mountain Dog. While the Bernese now registers respectable numbers—not too many, not too few—and is seen at dog shows all over North America, it was not always like this.

There was a time that the breed was an extreme rarity. Most people had never even heard of the breed, and their appearances at dog shows were few and far between, so dog fanciers were similarly unfamiliar with the "Berner."

All that has now changed, and it seems the dog Fancy and the larger world have finally discovered the breed and its abundance of wonderful attributes. We have seen the Bernese lend its photogenic presence to a variety of advertising messages in many kinds of media and we have also seen the breed as a companion highly regarded in large cities, country homes and everywhere in between.

Where the Berner was once a rare sight at a dog show, he is a regular winner at this time and makes a good account of himself in the Working Group and Best in Show ring. All these things augur well for the breed and its future. We are proud to have a part in the progress of the breed as evidenced by the appearance of *The*

New Bernese Mountain Dog. We hope that all friends of the breed will enjoy this fine new book by one of their own and make it a prime reference in their own dog book libraries. We further hope you will enjoy owning and using this book as we are proud to have produced it.

—The Publisher

About the Author

SHARON CHESNUTT SMITH is, in every sense, a Renaissance person in everything she does.

Born in Corpus Christi, Texas, Mrs. Smith was a member of a military family. As a small child, this circumstance kept her from realizing one of her most fervent dreams—owning a dog. In due course, however, she did own a succession of mixed breeds and purebreds. All formed in her an appreciation of what dogs add to our lives and our individual perceptions.

College and early career moves ruled out dog ownership during Mrs. Smith's early adulthood. Living in New York City, working for an airline and keeping dogs generally do not mix well.

Eventually a move to upstate New York made a lifelong dream an attainable reality, and with her husband, Sharon Smith began breeding Golden Retrievers with respectable success. In the keen competition of the Golden ring, the Smiths were able to finish seven homebreds and two dogs they purchased as their foundation stock. Unfortunately, the need to return to the world of business forced the Smiths to put the dog breeding venture on hold. But they were destined to become active again, this time with Bernese Mountain Dogs.

The author, Sharon Chesnutt Smith

The first Berner that the Smiths owned also became their first Best in Show winner and began a long, distinguished association with the breed. Today Sharon Chesnutt Smith and her husband maintain a small, select kennel now in its fifth generation of breeding under the October prefix.

Mrs. Smith is also a highly respected judge of Golden Retrievers and Bernese Mountain Dogs and currently serves as the delegate to the American Kennel Club from the Bernese Mountain Dog Club of America. She is also an active member of a number of all-breed dog clubs.

Outside the dog sport Mrs. Smith is in *Who's Who of American Women*, *The World's Who's Who of Women* and *Who's Who in Advertising*. She is a partner in the advertising agency Chesnutt & Smith, located in Catskill, New York. She has one son and her other interests include decorating, cooking and traveling.

With the publication of this book, it can truly be said of Sharon Chesnutt Smith that she has actively given to Bernese breeding at least what she has gotten from it, and probably even more.

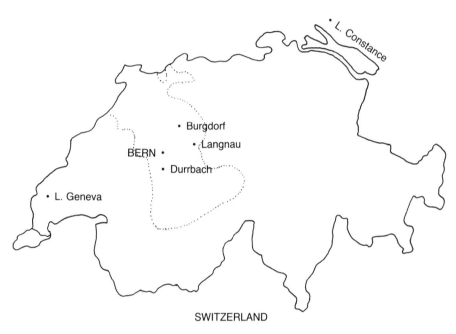

The canton of Bern is the place of origin of the Bernese Mountain Dog

1

Origins of the Bernese Mountain Dog

HISTORY

Bernese Mountain Dogs originated in Switzerland as farm dogs. Their ancestors are said to have appeared in Switzerland at the time of the Stone Age farmers of the Neolithic period (4000–1800 B.C.) These early farm dogs were the size of a medium "butcher dog" (or Rottweiller). Even though it has been believed for some time that these local farm dogs were probably crossbred with dogs introduced by invading Roman armies, recent research discloses that dogs the size of the modern Bernese Mountain Dog or Rottweiller were present long before occupation by Romans in this region. In fact, the latest studies find that the provincial populations of middle Europe were in no way altered by Roman influence and there are no reports that Roman soldiers even brought dogs with them!

Stories of Romans using dogs to guard and defend their watch-towers say nothing of these dogs' origins. They were probably recruited on site as were many professional soldiers.

Working dogs have always been important to the economy of the rural Swiss lifestyle. These two photos, taken in the early 1940s, clearly depict the interaction of people and dogs as it occurred for centuries before and even into our own time.

The uniformity of this group of dogs was brought about by the farmer's lifestyle. This area of the world developed uninterruptedly, both economically and culturally, thus allowing the development of a uniform type of dog.

The early Swiss farm dogs were used as guard and protection dogs, draft dogs for milkwagons and as helpers to the Alpine herders. Therefore, it was preferable to use dogs that did not posess marked hunting traits and instincts, but were strong and alert to protect against predatory animals. These qualities called for a large, strong dog that was both obedient and self-reliant. Since economic needs never threatened the area of Berne and farmers were generally prosperous, it follows that they could afford a stately, large courtyard dog. These dogs belonged to the farm and its property, and that is evidenced even today by the way a Bernese Mountain Dog greets his people to their property.

The Bernese is one of the four breeds of *Sennenhunde* (Alpine Herdsman's Dog). The four breeds were developed in several different regions of Switzerland. Giving rise to even more proof of the

It was not until almost the end of the nineteenth century that serious fanciers took notice of the remnants of the old Swiss farm dogs and began developing their potential for the showbench. Their early efforts and the work of those who followed have assured the Bernese Mountain Dog a secure place far into the future.

3

antiquity of these breeds was this division of the breeds according to geographical boundaries and regional use. The greater Swiss Mountain Dog being the oldest form, it is the one from which the other subgroups were developed. All four breeds have similar markings, but only the *Berner Sennenhunde* sports a long coat.

These four breeds are:

1. Appenzeller Sennenhunde—a midsized, short-haired dog with a ring tail, often carrying more white than the other three breeds (height at the shoulder, 19.5 to 21.5 inches)
2. Entlebucher Sennenhunde—a short-haired, small dog, with a stump tail (height at the shoulder, 15.5 to 17.5 inches)
3. Berner Sennenhunde (Bernese Mountain dog)—strong, mid-sized dog, long-haired (height at the shoulder, 23.5 to 25.5 inches)
4. Great Swiss Sennenhunde (Greater Swiss Mountain Dog)—short-haired, large size (height at the shoulder, 27.5 inches)

These Alpine herding dogs are the oldest living breeds in Switzerland, true Swiss national dogs. These native dogs were said to have been almost lost as new breeds were introduced and large groups of the population abandoned the old farm dogs for something special and new. The interest in breeds of other countries was heightened by a growing interest in the sport of dogs in the mid-1800s. Consequently, by 1870, the ordinary house or yard dogs were said to have all but vanished. Many records show that people began to notice the loss of this once-common breed. Older people spoke of the good old days of the ''four eyes'' (legend has it that superstitious people believed the spots over the eyes gave these dogs a second set of eyes to see ghosts) or ''yellow cheeks'' (*Gelbbackler*); since for centuries these dogs had no breed name, people of the region called them farm dogs, butcher's dogs, cheesery dogs or differentiated them according to markings. A dog with a wide white blaze was a *Blässi*, a dog with very little or no white was a *Bäire* (little bear) and a dog with a beautiful white collar forming around the neck was referred to as a *Ringgi* (ring around the neck). These early farm dogs remained unspoiled and pure in the upper mountain valleys in a region south of Berne, west of the Aaretal, between Aaretal and Schwarzwasser, known as the district of Dürrbach. People in the canton of Berne referred to the breed as the Dürrbachler—and here in 1890 these dogs could still be found hitched to milk carts, herding livestock, at cheese huts and pulling carts to market for nomadic basket weavers. In 1892 Franz Schertenleib bought one of these basket weaver's dogs; this was the first one of its kind seen in Burgdorf for many years. Later another fancier from Burgdorf purchased several more Dürrbachlers. The beginning of recognition as a breed came in 1899 when a Mr. Probst, the owner of a cafe in Berne, first brought to the fore the excellent character of the breed and pushed for a trial class at the International Swiss Kennel Club (SKG) show in 1904. The show held in Berne permitted this class. Mr. Probst judged and had an entry of seven—six dogs, one bitch. These dogs drew much attention and were soon entered into the Swiss Stud Book. The patriarchs of the breed were: Belline 1 2701, Ringgi 2700, Bäri 1, Prisca 3480, Sultan 3476, Prinz v. Burgdorf 3475, Nero 3474, Netty 3479, Bello Schertenleib 3473, Miss 3478.

In 1907, after a show in Lucerne, the *Schweizerische Dürrbachler Klub* was founded. Noted geologist and judge, Professor Albert Heim, asked this new club to promise "to take care of this noble breed in its sense and spirit, to provide for its notice, protection, recognition and distribution." Dr. Heim, the patriarch of the breed, also noted many problems that he felt the club should deal with. He noted that most of the tails were so strongly arched that they touched the back or actually laid on the back like that of a spitz type, and that the few hanging tails were much more beautiful and therefore more desirable. And the split nose! The farms of Seftigschwendi had a family of Bernese Mountain Dogs thought to be especially sharp and watchful because of their split noses. The people of Seftigschwendi considered this to be a true characteristic of the breed and the split-nosed dogs to be the real Dürrbachlers (one-quarter of the dogs entered in the show in Lucerne in 1907 had split noses). Dr. Heim considered this to be a conspicuous deformity rather than a purebred characteristic. This deformity causes the two nostrils to back up on one another and in severe cases continue into the gum area causing the incisor teeth to become arranged against one another, much like the so-called harelip in humans. The club eventually ruled to disown the split nose and the 1910 show in Burgdorf had only one split-nosed specimen in an entry of 107. Dr. Heim also noted the double dewclaws and suggested that they be removed to allow a free gait without interference by these useless appendages. He also asked that the light yellow or "eagle eyes" that gave those early farm dogs a wild expression be eliminated. In 1908, at the urging of Professor Heim, the name of the breed was changed to the *Berner Sennenhunde* (Bernese Alpine Herdsman Dog) to more closely follow the naming pattern of the other Sennenhunde, and the breed was officially recognized. The club then followed suit and was renamed the Berner Sennenhunde Club. In a few short years the breed began to receive much attention. The Swiss were very interested in this beautiful breed, native to their homeland. In 1910 a Specialty show for Berner Sennenhunden was held in Burgdorf. To attract breeding stock from a wide area and get a true picture, no entry fee was charged and very attractive prizes were offered. At this show judge Professor Albert Heim officiated over an entry of 107, and only eight were excused as "not purebred." Professor Heim recorded heights in his judging report at this show of "19 and ½ to 27 and ½," noting that many dogs were almost rectangular in appearance, with tails carried curled over the backs like the Appenzeller Mountain Dogs, and ninety-nine of the dogs were curly-coated and eight short-coated. Professor Heim was quite critical of the excessive height that distracted from the square sturdy look of the dog, and said of the curly coats: "the curly coat must disappear! It is not beautiful and not practical." This large entry (even by today's standards) was quite a gathering for a breed that is referred to in history as having been "almost lost" only a few years earlier. Was this breed truly "almost lost" or only hidden on distant isolated farms? This was the original melting pot of "farmer's dogs." By 1922, rising popularity in their homeland brought registrations in the Swiss Kennel Club to 58 for the year, and by 1939 they were up to 129. The Bernese was still very much a part of the melting pot at this time, with some still recorded as white-red in color.

THE ORIGINAL SWISS IMPORTS IN AMERICA

The Bernese Mountain Dog was officially recognized as a new breed in the Working Group by the American Kennel Club on April 12, 1937. This induction had its beginnings around 1926 when

Alex v. Angstorf, a well-known winner from the 1950s, came down from the New-foundland/Bernese cross as described in the text. Alex proved to have a significant impact on the breed, having sired fifty-one litters.

the farmer Isaac Schiess of Florence, Kansas, imported two Swiss Registry dogs: Donna von der Rothohe (female), and Poincare von Sumiswald (male). He tried to register this pair with the AKC to no avail; even the efforts of the Swiss Stud Book registrar were unsuccessful. A mating of Poincare and Donna produced a litter of five, whelped March 29, 1926, and although the litter was born in the United States, they could only be registered with the Swiss Kennel Club.

After reading an article entitled "The Bernese Is a Loyal Dog of the Swiss Alps," published in June 1935 in the AKC *Gazette* by Mrs. L. Egg-Leach, an English woman residing in Switzerland, the childhood yearnings of Mr. Glen Shadow, of Louisiana, were rekindled. He then began a long correspondence with Mrs. Egg-Leach discussing his early admiration of pictures showing these dogs drawing milk carts in his first grade reader. Taken with his correspondence she began her search for a female for him. Mrs. Egg-Leach was successful in finding CACIB Friday v. Haslenbach, who belonged to Mr. Fritz Stalder, her breeder. Friday was the best female of her breed at that time in all of Europe—making her purchase no small one. She was imported by Mr. Shadow in August 1936. In September of 1936, Mrs. Egg-Leach arranged for the import of Quell v. Tiergarten, also for Mr. Shadow. Quell was not the same fine quality of Friday, but was the best male available.

Although Mr. Shadow had several breeds, he had a deep admiration for the Bernese Mountain Dog.

MEANWHILE, BACK IN SWITZERLAND (OR, THE NEWFOUNDLAND INFLUENCE)

Although the early Bernese rescued from the farm valleys were outcrossed as much as possible with known, available breeding stock, by the late 1940s it was felt necessary to introduce new blood, possibly to clean up some shy, poor temperaments, since many of the old farmers had selectively bred for insecure, aggressive temperaments. These temperaments were considered good for watchdogs on remote farms where framers allowed them to roam free at night warding off any wandering vagabonds.

A supposed accidental breeding of a Bernese female, Christine v. Lux, to a Newfoundland dog, Pluto v. Erlengut, ended all discussion of which breed would be most suitable. One cannot help but wonder if this mating was not struck in response to Dr. Heim's discussion of Bernese in 1914, and I quote:

> There are slight Newfoundlands that are very close to the Bernese Mountain Dog in their total form, although usually they have the more elegant, correct movement in the hind feet, since they lack double dewclaws. The head of the Bernese Mountain Dog also is reminiscent of the beautiful noble head of a light, slender Newfoundland. If I were to paint on the latter the white and red markings, then it would be almost the ideal head of a Bernese Mountain Dog.

This Newfoundland cross produced a litter of seven on December 21, 1948. Pluto v. Elrengut, a purebred Newfoundland, bred Christine v. Lux, a purebred female Bernese Mountain Dog. One female from this mating, Babette, with traditional Newfoundland looks and temperament (all black, little white on chin and toes), was bred to a pure Bernese male named Aldo v. Tieffurt. On March 23, 1951, she had a litter of eight puppies. One male and female were marked like a Bernese, but the male had no white markings on the hind feet. The female named Christine v. Schwarzwasserbachli was later bred to a pure Bernese male, Osi v. Allenuften, on March 15, 1952. Christine delivered five puppies—all marked like Bernese! So from 1948 to 1952, just four short years, the cross was complete, leaving behind a legacy of better depth of chest, a shiny black, straight coat and improved temperament. There were two dogs of this final litter that were bred, Alex v. Angstorf (male) and Bella v. Angstorf (female). Bella was mated to Dana v. Enggistein and produced a litter of eight, all Bernese. Unfortunately, Bella was put to sleep at four years of age so her influence was not great. Alex v. Angstorf went on to become an international and world champion—and it was he who influenced the breed the most by siring fifty-one litters—quite an impact.

Although it is said that the Swiss very rarely linebred, today there are kennels linebreeding and inbreeding on stock that goes back to Alex, as are many kennels in the United States—and as yet, no Newfoundlands! Considering this dog's sweeping influence on the breed it is quite amazing, but the true Swiss breed won out. However, Alex did much to establish the breed and very few if any Swiss as well as American lines do not go back to him or his sister.

That which is instinctive is never lost. Here "Kandi" pulls a cart loaded with hay as owner Mrs. Arthur Harberts, pitchfork in hand, walks alongside the hard-working Berner. Six-year-old Rita Hutchins, in an authentic Swiss farm work costume, lends additional authenticity to the scene. *Josef Scaylea,* The Seattle Times

2

The Development of the Breed in the United States

THE EARLY DOGS AND THEIR BREEDERS

Up to 1949, Mr. Glen Shadow was the only owner/breeder of AKC registered Bernese Mountain Dogs in America. He was very enthusiastic about the breed and expresses his feelings in an article where he wrote:

> Anyone looking into these dogs' deep brown eyes can see that they have a wonderful understanding and a kind, loving disposition. They are most affectionate toward children and are quite courageous in defending their rights. As a working dog, I have never seen one that I think equals the Bernese dog and if the homes that have suffered the loss of children from vicious kidnappers had had one of these dogs as a pet and pal for their child, no one would have been able to molest them without first killing the dog.

Quite a testimonial to a wonderful breed. This kind of enthusiasm enabled Mr. Shadow to achieve the recognition of the breed by the American Kennel Club.

In 1949, 1950 and 1951, three more people imported dogs from Switzerland: Robert M. Youngs, Stewart G. Mayse and Yvonne Auer—but no litters resulted.

Those early years were very different from today: shipping dogs was much more difficult, air travel was long and pretty rough and sea travel was even worse. Breeding over long distances was an incredible time consumer and economically unfeasible. World War II put a stop to all importing for quite a few years.

After 1954, registrations picked up somewhat, and in 1959 a Swiss woman living in Vermont, Nelly Frey, bred her female, Lory v. Sunnehuebeli, to Banz v. d. Kuhweid. From this litter came Aya

Rita Hutchins provides the Harbertses' puppies with some invaluable socialization. Note the markings on the chests of these puppies bear an amazing resemblance to the white cross emblazoned on the Swiss flag.

Josef Scaylea, The Seattle Times

"Judi" and "Bobi" have been trained to perform as pack dogs by the Hutchinses to develop them as useful additions to hunting and fishing expeditions.

Josef Scaylea, The Seattle Times

of Verlap, owned by M. A. and William Horstick, who became the first Bernese to gain an Obedience title, and Anna of Arlboden, owned by the Pickerings of Washington state, who was the second CD (but not until 1965). Information is vague until 1962 when nine owners were listed with the AKC. In the south they were Dr. C. Walter Mattingly in Louisiana and Dr. Judge M. Lyle in Texas, and in the upper Midwest, Bishop W. W. Horstick and his daughter, Mary Alice. Mary Alice is still active in the breed today as Mary Alice Eschweiler.

The strongest concentration of the nine was in the Pacific Northwest. These enthusiasts included Dr. and Mrs. Arthur Harberts, Mr. and Mrs. Charles Hutchins, Mr. and Mrs. Harold Thompson and Mrs. Bea Knight. These owners worked together to promote

Beatrice Knight shown here in a mid-1970s photograph with a Bernese puppy and surrounded by a group of Mrs. Knight's adoring Saint Bernards. Mrs. Knight was very close to being a legendary figure for her Sanctuary Woods Saint Bernards and later Bernese Mountain Dogs.

Lorna Felice

the breed. The Hutchinses and the Harbertses were featured in a *Seattle Sunday Times* rotogravure on May 13, 1962, entitled "A Bit of Bern Near Bothell." This article features Mrs. Harberts and the three pups from her dogs Kandi and Cina, the first litter born in the state of Washington, and also shows the Hutchinses with Bobi and Judy. Bobi is none other than Bobi v. Bauernheim. Judy was purchased from one of the early Southern breeders, Dr. Judge M. Lyle.

Flott v. d. Waldheimat
CACIB Ch. Zorro v. Muhlstein
Cora v. Viererfeld
Bobi v. Bauerheim
Eiger v. Munnenberg
Madi v. Munnenberg
Heidi v. Munnenberg

Bella's Albertine, Axel, Angelique

CACIB Ch. Alex v. Angstorf
Casar v. Niederwangen
Erna v. Muhlekopf
Bella v. Moosboden
Ador v. Liselisbrunneli
Beline v. Schneggenberg
Extra v. Diessbachfluh

Pedigree "A"

Bobi and Judy produced Ch. Tabea of Altadena. Bobi was also bred to Harold and Jane Thompson's import, Bella v. Mooseboden (a granddaughter of Alex v. Angstorf) just once, this mating producing Bella's Axel, Bella's Angelique and Bella's Albertine. (Thus began the well-known Bella line.) The Thompsons then imported Arno v. d. Grasburg in 1967, who was a linebreeding on CACIB Ch. Alex v. Angstorf in the third and fourth generation, and bred him to Bella's Albertine, who also had Alex in the fourth generation. This combination produced the first champion in Washington state, Bella's Caesar, Bella's Clara (who will appear in many pedigrees of outstanding dogs to come) and B. Albertine's George.

15

Bari v. d. Holzmuhle
Dursli v. d. Holzmuhle
Mudi v. Bandis
Dani v. Ried
Cowboy v. d. Gotthlfsegg
Diane v. Bernerland
Cornelia v. Wallzcherhof
Ultra v. Oberfeld
Bari v. d. Holzmuhle
Dursli v. d. Holzmuhle
Mudi v. Bradis
Dorette v. Schwandelirain
CACIB Ch. Alex v. Angstorf
Greta v. Munnenberg
Dori v. Munnenberg

Sanctuary Woods Black Litter

Flott v. d. Waldheimat
CACIB Ch. Zorro v. Muhlstein
Cora v. Viererfeld
Dani v. Senseboden
CACIB Ch. Alex v. Angstorf
Berna v. Burgistein
Bella v. Nyffelhof
Gretel v. Langmoos
Arno v. Pfrund
Toni v. Oberbottigen
Sonja v. Oberbottigen
Flocki v. Laupenacker
Kuno v. Sunnehubel
Janette v. Schlossi
Hella v. Schlossi

16

Pedigree "B"

Mrs. Bea Knight of Drain, Oregon, who had been breeding Saint Bernards under the kennel name of Sanctuary Woods since 1946, imported a pair of Berners but was unsuccessful in breeding them. Mrs. Knight later imported two more females as breeding stock. One of these, Gretel v. Langmoos (a great granddaughter of Alex v. Angstorf), was mated to the Horstick's male Ultra v. Oberfeld "Freddy" (also a great-grandson of Alex v. Angstorf), who was loaned to Mrs. Knight for breeding purposes. They produced a litter of eleven pups on April 19, 1966. This was the well-known Sanctuary Woods "Black" litter.

The first and second champions in the United States resulted from this litter: Ch. Sanctuary Woods Black Knight, owned by Roberta Subin, and Ch. Sanctuary Woods Black Lancer, owned by his breeder, Bea Knight.

This combination of Ultra v. Oberfeld (who was the result of a linebreeding on Dursli v. Holzmuhle), and Gretel v. Langmoos, was a loose linebreeding (fourth generation) on CACIB Ch. Alex v. Angstorf (the result of the Newfoundland cross).

This combination also contained CACIB Ch. Zorro v. Muhlstein, the grandfather of the Bella line. Thus these two breedings, as well as Bobi ex Judy, opened up a wealth of linebreeding possibilities, and many budding young kennels took advantage of them as did Bea Knight, who was already quite knowledgeable and well established in the Saint Bernard world. I have heard it said by many Saint Bernard breeders that Bea Knight could sit ringside and pick out every Saint in the ring that went back to Sanctuary Woods stock (even if it was in the fifth generation) and never be wrong.

Bella's Clara, bred by the Thompsons, eventually ended up in the Midwest with Martha Decker and Sylvia Howison. Bella fit right into an already established breeding program. The Howisons had imported Ch. Wendy v. d. Grasburg (the first Bernese to receive an OFA #1), who was a linebreeding on Alex v. Angstorf and the very same breeding as Arno v. d. Grasburg. Wendy was bred to Casar v. Oberbottigen, who had Alex in his fourth generation and CACIB Ch. Zorro v. Muhlstein in the third, owned by William Periera of Ohio (OFA #4). Everyone was linebreeding on Zorro and Alex in those early years, even the Swiss. Why not? After all, these two dogs held the CACIB title, which is the highest champion certificate on the continent of Europe, known as the International Beauty Championship Certificate.

Showing was very frustrating in those early years. Competition was nearly impossible to find and Group judges were unsure of this rare breed. This was noted by the Horsticks in 1965 when the Group judge at a large show approached them after judging and commented, "This is a beautiful dog and I was very tempted to place him in the Group. But I have never seen one before and don't know what they should look like."

Then a breakthrough! On November 6, 1966, Sanctuary Woods Black Knight, owned by Roberta Subin and bred by Bea Knight, walked away with a fourth place in the Working Group at the Riverside Kennel Club show, winning the first 3-point major in the history of the breed, and later became the first AKC Bernese champion. Black Knight along with his brother Black Lancer formed the first Bernese Brace to be shown. Sanctuary Woods Black Knight was later purchased by Alpstein kennel in Ohio and although he lived a relatively short life, sired several litters.

Pedigrees "C" and "D"

Mrs. Knight bred Bella's Axel (a son of Bobi ex Bella) to her Gretel v. Langmoos, thus doubling up on CACIB Ch. Zorro v. Muhlstein and producing Ch. Sanctuary Woods Gordo, the first Bernese to win first place in the Working Group. Gordo was an outstanding show dog who did a great deal of winning in his time and did much to popularize the breed.

Gordo was one of the foundation dogs of another kennel that still linebreeds on that original stock today, Mon Plaisir, headed by Susanne Gagnon in New Jersey.

Mrs. Knight also bred her female Gretel back to one of Gretel's sons from that first "Black" litter. A female from this inbred litter, Mon Plaisir's Enchantress, was acquired by the Gagnons and, in turn, was bred to Gordo. The product of this tight linebreeding was then bred to the Gagnon's imported male, Beatus v. d. Froburg (himself a loose linebreeding on Carlo v. d. Grandfeybrucke), and this combination produced Ch. Mon Plaisir's Shady Lady, CDX, in April 1974. Shady Lady was used extensively by Gale Werth of

Broken Oaks kennel in Wisconsin. She produced Specialty winners and High in Trial (HIT) winners.

I could go on and on tracing dogs back to these five original dogs and their relatives, as well as their closely related imported mates. In sections on specific dogs such as the Best in Show dogs, I will note the dogs related to these early breedings. I believe you will find it fascinating that almost every early kennel, with very few exceptions, started their breeding programs with dogs out of or closely related to these early breedings. And why not? The first champions and Group-placing dogs as well as some of the first hip clearances came from these dogs. That first Sanctuary Woods litter also contained eleven puppies, so there were lots to go around for a rare breed.

I remember standing outside the Bernese ring at a show many years ago and having an acquaintance from another breed walk up and say, "Do you have one of these?" (meaning a Bernese) and when I replied, "Yes," they remarked, "Oh, well, you'll do great in this breed with your background in linebreeding. These people (meaning Bernese breeders) haven't got a clue—they always out-cross!" Well, that certainly wasn't true in the sixties and early seventies. Perhaps more recent outcrossing were in response to all the earlier linebreeding and inbreeding! But then everything old is always new again. Currently, linebreeding and inbreeding are once again very popular.

By 1966 owners and breeders were able to contact each other through American Kennel Club records and advertising. The number of registrations had moved out of the teens, no doubt helped by Gretel's litter of eleven in April of that year. By 1972 registrations were approaching the 200 mark. The breed was finally on its way!

THE BEGINNING OF THE BERNESE MOUNTAIN DOG CLUB OF AMERICA

Carol Pyle was introduced to Bernese by Bea Knight, when she made a trip to Oregon to look at Sanctuary Woods Saint Bernards and inquired as to the name of the "other breed." At that time Mrs. Knight had two Bernese named Stranger and Tiptoes that she had purchased from a doctor in Texas (Dr. Lyle). She commented that she had had no luck breeding them and was looking into importing

Flott v. d. Waldeimat
CACIB Ch. Zorro v. Muhlstein
Cora v. Viererfeld
Bobi v. Bauerheim
Eiger v. Munnenberg
Madi v. Munnenberg
Heidi v. Munnenberg
Bella's Axel
CACIB Ch. Alex v. Angstorf
Casar v. Niederwangen
Erna v. Muhlekopf
Bella v. Moosboden
Ador v. Liselisbruneli
Beline v. Schneggenberg
Extra v. Diessbachfluh

Ch. Sanctuary Woods Gordo

Flott v. d. Waldheimat
CACIB Ch. Zorro v. Muhlstein
Cora v. Viererfeld
Dani v. Senseboden
CACIB Ch. Alex v. Angstorf
Berna v. Burgistein
Bella v. Nyffelhof
Gretel v. Langmoos
Arno v. Pfrund
Toni v. Oberbottigen
Sonya v. Oberbottigen
Flocki v. Laupenacker
Kuno v. Sunnehubel
Janette v. Schlossi
Hella v. Schlossi

20

Ch. Sanctuary Woods Gordo, owned by Joseph and Susanne Gagnon and bred by Beatrice Knight, was the first of the breed to place first in the Working Group.

Carlo v. d. Grandfeybrucke
Astor v. Chaindon
Diana v. Ruegsbach
Porthos LaVaux
CACIB York v. Fluhwald
Anita v. Blasenwald
Lanca v. d. Gotthelfsegg
Beatus v. d. Froburg
CACIB Alex v. Bauerheim
Bari v. d. Taubenfluh
Eve v. d. Klostealp
Era v. Chaindon
Carlo v. d. Grandfeybrucke
Bella v. Chaindon
Diana v. Ruegsbach

Ch. Mon Plaisir's Shady Lady

Bobi v. Bauerheim
Bella's Axel
Bella v. Moosboden
Ch. Sanctuary Woods Gordo
Dani v. Senseboden
Gretel v. Langmoos
Flocki v. Laupenacker
Mon Plaisir's Enchantress
Ultra v. Oberfeld
Ch. Sanctuary Woods Black Lancer
Gretel v. Langmoos
Mon Plaisir's Reine Royale
Dani v. Senseboden
Gretel v. Langmoos
Flocki v. Laupenacker

Ch. Mon Plaisir's Shady Lady, owned by Gale Werth, was a granddaughter of "Gordo" and was an important factor in her owner's Broken Oaks Kennels as the producer of Specialty and HIT winners.

American Kennel Club Registrations (1937–1972)

Year	Registered	Year	Registered
1937	2	1957	6
1938	1	1958	0
1939	0	1959	7
1940	8	1960	10
1941–44	0	1961	7
1945	0	1962	4
1946	1	1963	6
1947	1	1964	11
1948	7	1965	17
1949	2	1966	31
1950	1	1967	22
1951	2	1968	43
1952	0	1969	59
1953	2	1970	103
1954	5	1971	152
1955	3	1972	185
1956	3		

a pair. Mrs. Pyle some years later purchased a puppy from one of these two imports, Gretel. This pup, Sanctuary Woods Color Scheme, was out of Gretel's second litter with the Thompsons' male Bella's Axel. Color Scheme was a littermate to Copyright and Cloud Nine who both became champions along with Charm who earned her CD. The repeat of this breeding produced Gordo.

Carol and several others on the West Coast decided to form a breed club in the summer of 1967 in order to keep in touch with others who owned this wonderful breed. The American Kennel Club helped them locate owners, and by January of 1968 at the Golden Gate show in San Francisco, two Bernese were entered for the first time. Information was handed out on the fledging club and eight members were present: Mr. and Mrs. Fred (Carol) Pyle, Mr. Howard

Brown, Mr. Gordon Loveless, Miss Roberta Subin, Mrs. Ruth Hug and Mr. and Mrs. Francis Lockhart.

Mrs. Pyle followed up this meeting with the first club newsletter in March of the same year.

With membership soaring to thirty-three, May of that year saw the appointment of pro-tempore officers: president, Howard Brown; vice president, Ruth Hug; secretary/treasurer, Carol Pyle.

By 1969 the club held its first election of officers: president, Dr. Mary Dawson; vice president, Harold Howison; treasurer, F. M. Lockhart; secretary, Carol Pyle; board members—Penny Buchanan, Barbara Gold, William Hall, Bea Knight, Barbara Packard. The newsletter editor was Carol Pyle. Membership had soared to seventy. The first fun match was held in 1970 in California; this began a long-standing tradition of Bernese-only matches known as "Bernerfests." In July of that year the Santa Barbara show had a record entry of eleven Bernese. This was the very first 5-point major in the breed. The show was judged by Major Godsol, who awarded those points to Hektor v. d. Klosteralp and Bella v. Nesselacker, both owned by Fritz Gautschi. The other dogs entered were Sanctuary Woods Copyright, Sanctuary Woods Cloud Nine, Sanctuary Woods Gloriann (Gordo's sister), Sanctuary Woods Early Bird (all of these dogs and Hektor became champions). Of the other six entries two died before they could finish. The other entries were Sanctuary Woods Go Boy, Sablemate Mountaineer, Abbe-Girl of the Alps, Sanctuary Woods Delsa and Sanctuary Woods Ilona.

In 1972 the club was officially incorporated as the Bernese Mountain Dog Club of America or BMDCA. Things still moved at a snail's pace. The numbers of dogs being shown were very small; often people had to call friends to get together and bring enough dogs to build a major, or if a couple of fair-sized kennels got together, they could build their own major. From 1968 to 1973 a total of eighty titles were completed.

The Bernese Mountain Dog Club of America was given permission from the American Kennel Club in the spring of 1972 to hold its first sanctioned (B) match. In 1974 the first AO-A match was held, and the second AO-A match in Pennsylvania gave the BMDCA AKC "licensed" status. The club was now ready to host its own Specialty shows. The first National Specialty for Bernese

Mountain Dogs in the United States was held in Harrisburg, Pennsylvania, in 1976.

SPECIALTY WINNERS

The first Specialty in Harrisburg, Pennsylvania, boasted seventy-one dogs in competition and was judged by Mr. Arnold Woolf on March 13, 1976. Mr. Woolf commented that three-quarters of the dogs shown to him moved too wide in the front and were extremely straight in the shoulder. This show set a precedent that has never since been repeated: Best of Breed went to Dr. Mary Dawson's bitch Ch. Zyta v. Nesselacker. Zyta was and still remains the only bitch to ever win the Best of Breed trophy at a National Specialty despite all the discussion year after year about better overall quality in the bitch classes. Best of Opposite Sex was awarded to Ch. Goliath v. Zinggen. Both winners were Swiss imports. Registrations for 1976 reached 292 and membership in the BMDCA reached 300.

In April 1977 the National Specialty moved to the West Coast. There were fifty-seven dogs in competition and registrations of Bernese in America were up to 324. At this Specialty a breeder/judge and club member, Esther Mueller, presided. Her choice for Best of Breed was a dog destined to be the first Best in Show dog in the history of the breed, Ch. Alphorn's Copyright of Echo. Copyright was a true link to those early breedings and the first dogs in the Pacific Northwest. As such his pedigree is also noteworthy.

Mrs. Mueller awarded Best of Opposite Sex to Ch. Car-Mar's A-Miss v. Copyright; she was also a product of the same type of linebreeding based on Sanctuary Woods stock. Her father was out of Axel ex Gretel and her mother was a tight linebreeding on Ultra v. Oberfeld.

This was truly a show for the "Copyrights" of those original dogs!

The very first Independent National Specialty hosted by the BMDCA was held in Pontiac, Michigan, on May 20, 1978. This Specialty brought out eighty-eight dogs for the evaluation of the late Mrs. Maynard "Kitty" Drury. Mrs. Drury commented that finding type and soundness was a challenge, but overall she judged

This interesting photo, taken at the 1979 BMDCA Specialty, includes three generations of historically significant dogs and the fanciers they are associated with. Ch. Zyta v. Nesselacker (far right) was the winner of the breed's first Specialty. She is handled by her owner, Mary Dawson. Left of Zyta is her mate, Ch. Jean Henri LaVaux, handled by owner Mary Alice (Horstick) Eschweiler. The next dog, Ch. Dagne v. Hexliheim, is by Jean Henri out of Zyta. She is handled by Christina Ohlsen. At Dagne's left is her mate, Ch. Wyemede's Luron Bruce, handled by his owner Claudia Buss, and their three offspring: Ch. Shepard's Patch Carl B, handled by owner Deborah Mulvey; Shepard's Patch Cartier, handled by Deborah Godfrey; and Shepard's Patch Chemarain (handler unidentified). Such photo records allow better understanding of families and dogs that might otherwise just be names on pedigrees.

on soundness. Once again Best of Breed was awarded to the Johnsons' Copyright. The Johnsons were also Saint Bernard breeders, and it is interesting that the breed seems to owe a great deal to the Saint Bernard world. Best of Opposite Sex was awarded to Ch. Gina v. Zinggen, an import (from the Veterans class) and a litter sister to Ch. Goliath v. Zinggen, the BOS winner at the first Specialty. Mrs. Drury's judging was truly a combination of the first two Specialties.

The Specialty returned to the East, to Bethlehem, Pennsylvania, on April 28, 1979. This year's judge, Mr. C. Seaver Smith, presided over a record number of dogs in competition—157. Mr.

Dani v. Reid
Ultra v. Oberfeld
Dorette v. Schwandelirain
Ch. Sanctuary Woods Black Knight
Dani v. Senseboden
Gretel v. Langmoos
Flocki v. Laupenacker
Ch. Trarr Alphorn Knight Echo
Kilian v. Engglsteln
Ch. Hector v. Nesselacker
Flora v. Nesselacker
Ch. Tryarr Conspiratess
Arno v. d. Grasburg
Bella's Clara
Bella's Albertine

Ch. Alphorn's Copyright of Echo

Galen v. Mattenhof
Ch. Klaus v. Kiesenthal
Tilla v. Quellbach
Ch. Clara's Christopher
Arno v. d. Grasburg
Bella's Clara
Bella's Albertine
Ch. Tryarr Alphorn Brio
Ultra v. Oberfeld
Ch. Sanctuary Woods Black Knight
Gretel v. Langmoos
Alpsteins Knight Dream
Casar v. Oberbottigen
Bonne Amie
Ch. Wendy v. d. Grasburg

Ch. Alphorn's Copyright of Echo (Ch. Tryarr Alphorn Knight Echo ex Ch. Tryarr Alphorn Brio), bred and owned by Dr. and Mrs. D. G. Johnson, was a BIS winner, a national Specialty winner and the sire of eleven champions, including three BMDCA Specialty Best of Breed winners. *Don Petrulis*

Smith spoke of the overall lovely entry, superb temperaments, pleasant people and great surroundings. He found the problem areas to be shoulders, wide fronts, tight, curly coats and less than level toplines. He awarded Best of Breed to Ch. Halidom Davos v. Yodlerhof, CD. Davos was destined to become the breed's all-time top producer of champions and Obedience title holders. Best of Opposite Sex went to Ch. Martha's Teddy Bear, CD, TD (from the Veteran bitch class); both these dogs also go back to the early dogs. Teddy Bear's dam was Bella's Clara and her sire was Ch. Hector v. Nesselacker, a Zorro grandson. Davos's sire was out of the very same sire and dam as Teddy Bear and his dam was an import

Ch. Goliath v. Zinggen (Graf v. Barenried ex Evi v. Zinggen), owned by James Curtiss and bred by C. Frankhauser, was Best of Opposite Sex at the first BMDCA Specialty and the breed's fourth Group winner. *Bushman*

linebred on CACIB Ch. Alex v. Bauernheim who had the same dam as Bobi v. Bauernheim and Madi v. Munnenberg.

The Specialty was back on the West Coast in 1980, at Santa Rosa, California, on April 19. Judge James T. Bennett presided over eighty-seven dogs. This year's selection for Best of Breed was Ch. Ashley v. Bernerliebe, CD. Back to the same early dogs? You bet! Ashley's dam was a littermate to Davos, the 1979 winner. Ashley's sire was Ch. Galan v. Senseboden, who was imported from Switzerland, along with his sister Ch. Ginger v. Senseboden (Davos's dam), by Jim Brooks in August 1973. So, to sum it up, Ashley's sire was his granddam's brother, making him a three-quarter inbreeding, with the addition of Ch. Grand Yodler of Teton Valley, CDX, whose mother was Bella's Clara. Best of Opposite Sex went to Jim Brook's Ch. Doska v. Yodlerhof, a littermate to Davos.

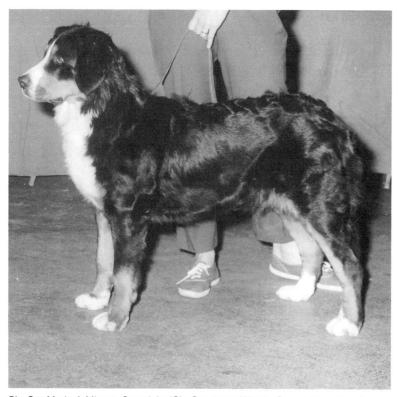

Ch. Car-Mar's A-Miss v. Copyright (Ch. Sanctuary Woods Copyright ex Sanctuary Woods Ebony Miss), owned and bred by Carolyn and Marty Lockhart, was a successful show dog as well as a producer. *Bennett Associates*

The 1981 Specialty took place in Oak Creek, Wisconsin, in May. This Specialty was the first to include a licensed Tracking test. Mrs. Bernard Freeman presided over an entry of eighty-one dogs. Her choice for Best of Breed was Ch. Maren's Ajax, whose father was a two-time Specialty winner, Ch. Alphorn's Copyright of Echo. Ajax's mother was Ch. Clara's Blass, back to those early dogs on both sides! Best of Opposite was awarded to Ch. Broken Oaks Bergita, CDX, TD, Bda. CD. Her dam was from one of the early Mon Plaisir breedings and her sire was Ch. Darius of Rutherford, whose maternal grandsire was Bruno v. Bauernheim, Bobi v. Bauernheim's brother, and whose sire's great-granddam was Bella's Albertine out of Bobi and Bella.

Ch. Gina v. Zinngen (Graf v. Barenried ex Evi v. Zinggen), a Swiss import owned by Esther Mueller and bred by C. Frankhauser, was BOS at the first independent Specialty of the BMDCA scoring from the Veterans' class. *William P. Gilbert*

Mrs. Freeman's comments were based more on the actual dogs she judged than the breed in general. But she did mention that any poor temperaments were not considered, as she feels this is paramount in a large working dog. She also noted that she felt cosmetic faults were less important than working faults. To further explain this she defined markings as cosmetic faults and inverted eyelids as working faults since they render a dog useless.

The May 1982 Specialty was held in Oswego, New York. By this time individual Bernese registrations in the United States had reached 424, 101 litters were produced and show entries were reflecting this growth. The Specialty judge was Mr. Melbourne Downing, and his entry was 141 dogs. Once again Ch. Ashley v. Bernerliebe walked off with the Best of Breed trophy and Best of Opposite Sex was awarded to Ch. Tails N Hock Tasha of Black Mt.

Ch. Halidom Davos v. Yodlerhof, CD (Ch. Grand Yodler of Teton Valley, CDX ex Ch. Ginger v. Senseboden), bred by James G. Brooks and owned by Millicent Buchanan Parliman. Davos is the breed's top producer, having sired 44 conformation champions and 19 obedience title holders. He was also BB at the 1979 BMDCA Specialty. *John Ashbey*

By now the end of April or mid-May had become the traditional time of year for the Specialty. The 1983 Specialty was held in Issaquah, Washington, on May 22. The judge was Marian Hodesson, and there were eighty dogs in competition. Best of Breed was once again Ch. Ashley v. Bernerliebe, CD, the only Bernese to date to ever win the Specialty three times. Best of Opposite Sex was awarded to Ch. Tauna's Lady Silvertip.

The 1984 Specialty show was held in Romulus, Michigan, on May 12 and 13. An entry of 133 dogs turned out for breeder/judge Gretchen Johnson. Mrs. Johnson's choice for Best of Breed was Ch. Broken Oaks Dieter v. Arjana, CD, who once again traced back tightly on the early dogs. His dam's parents were Ch. Alphorn's Copyright of Echo and Ch. Mon Plaisir's Shady Lady. His sire, Ch. Wyemede's Luron Bruce, went back to Black Lancer in the fourth generation. Mrs. Johnson's choice for Best of Opposite Sex

Ch. Ashley v. Bernerliebe, CD (Ch. Galan v. Senseboden ex Ch. Dult Daphne v. Yodlerhof), owned and bred by Joel and Christina Ohlsen. This three-time Specialty BB winner was also a top producer with 28 conformation champions and 14 obedience titlists to his credit.

Ch. Doska v. Yodlerhof, owned by Robert and Avis Ranck, was a litter sister to Davos and Dult Daphne. She was BOS at the 1980 BMDCA Specialty.

Ch. Maren's Ajax (Ch. Alphorn's Copyright of Echo ex Ch. Clara's Blass), owned by Loyal and Lori Jodar and bred by Marcus and Janice Ahrens, was BB at the 1981 BMDCA Specialty.   *Martin Booth*

was Ch. Roundtop's Abigail, also related back to the early dogs heritage of Alex.

The 1985 Specialty was held in the East. The dates were May 18 and 19 in Parsippany, New Jersey. Once again the breeder/judge was Mrs. Esther Mueller for bitches and intersex and Dr. Richard Greathouse for the dog classes. Yes, the entry of 223 had reached the point of needing two judges if they were to be judged in one day. Mrs. Mueller chose Can. Ch. Bigpaws Yoda for Winners Dog, Best of Winners and Best of Breed (the first Canadian dog to win the Specialty). The Best of Opposite Sex award went to Broken Oak's I-Ching, scoring from the Bred by Exhibitor class. Her sire was, once again, Ch. Wyemede's Luron Bruce, and her dam was a Shady Lady daughter.

The 1986 Specialty returned to California, and this year's

Ch. Tails N Hock Tasha of Black Mt. (Am., Can. Ch. Fidoberg ex Tails N Hock Bright Hope), owned by Deborah Mulvey and Carolann Schmid and bred by Carol Lavell, was BOS at the 1982 BMDCA Specialty. *Stephen Klein*

judge, Mr. James T Bennett, presided over 146 dogs. His Best of Breed winner was Ch. Shersan Chang O'Pace v. Halidom, CD. "Pace" was and still remains the biggest-winning Bernese in the history of the breed. He was also from that original legacy and was, in fact, line bred on Bella's Clara. Best of Opposite came from the classes—she was a Canadian entry, Can. Ch. Gitana De Braye, CD.

Mrs. Bernard Freeman returned to judge the Specialty in Waukesha, Wisconsin, on Mother's Day 1987. The entry of 141 dogs and the extreme heat challenged Mrs. Freeman in several ways. She was, however, equal to the challenges she faced and came up with another Canadian dog for Best of Breed, Can. & Am. Ch. Harlaquin's Thor the Bear. Best of Opposite Sex went to Ch. Borendale

Ch. Tauna's Lady Silvertip (Ch. Pike's Harpo J. Andrew ex Ch. Bernley's Bacardi of Pike), owned by Beverly Search and bred by James Smalley. This Berner was the breed's number one bitch for 1984 and was BOS at the 1983 Specialty.

Lewis Roberts

Puffin v. Ledgewood, whose grandfather was Ashley and great grandmother was Shady Lady. Registrations in the United States that year hit 862, and 215 litters were recorded, along with 101 championship titles.

The 1988 Specialty was held in Stowe, Vermont, in a uniquely beautiful setting, very much like being transported to the Swiss Alps. This was the ideal backdrop for the 20th Anniversary show. The judge, Mrs. Helen Miller Fisher, came from the world of German Shepherds. Side movement ruled the day, and since it was extremely hot, any dog and handler that could race in the heat had the advantage. There were 224 dogs in competition and the show was held over two days. Mrs. Fisher's Best of Breed winner was an Ashley son from Arizona, Am. & Can. Ch. DeerPark Heartlight, and Best of Opposite Sex went once again to the class bitch from Canada, Can. Ch. Gitana De Braye.

The next year, 1989, saw another hot Specialty in Phoenix,

Ch. Broken Oaks Dieter v. Arjana, CD (Ch. Wyemede's Luron Bruce ex Ch. Broken Oaks Arjana, CD), owned and bred by Gale Werth, was BB at the 1984 BMDCA Specialty and was the sire of 19 champions.   *Stephen Klein*

Ch. Roundtop's Abigail (Ch. Fels v. Muenterplatz ex Ch. Roundtop's Daphne v. Hexilheim), owned by Mary Jo and Mary Beth Thomson and bred by William and Mary Jo Thomson, was BOS at the 1984 BMDCA Specialty under breeder/judge Gretchen Johnson.   *Martin Booth*

Am., Can. Ch. Bigpaws Yoda (Can. Ch. Bari v. Nydegghoger ex Can. Ch. Kala vom Breiterweg), owned and bred by Susan Quinn, was the first Canadian dog to win the BMDCA Specialty. The year was 1985.
Purebred photos

Ch. Broken Oaks I Ching (Ch. Wye-mede's Luron Bruce ex Ch. Broken Oaks Butik, CD), owned and bred by Gale Werth, was BOS at the 1985 BMDCA Specialty. *Kohler*

Ch. Harlaquin's Thor the Bear (Valleyvu's Teddy Bear ex Harlequin's Brit the Sky-watcher), owned by Gina M. Donnell and bred by Kim Kilroy, was BB at the BMDCA 1987 Specialty and is further distin-guished as a top producer.

Am., Can. Ch. Deerpark Heartlight (Ch. Ashley v. Bernerliebe, CD ex Deepark Daisy), owned by Denise Dean and co-bred by her with Lisa Curtis. The top conformation dog of 1987 and 1988, he was the sire of forty-two champions and was BB at the BMDCA Specialty in 1988. *Carl Lindemaier*

39

Am., Can. Ch. Alpenblick's Alpine Alpenweide, CD (Ch. Pike's Harpo v. Andrew ex Ch. Alpenweide's Alpha Heidi, CDX), owned by Phillip and Donna Harness and bred by David and Coral Denis, was the first of the breed to win both the American and Canadian national Specialty shows. *Kohler*

Arizona. The show was held early in April but the temperature still registered 100 degrees, tough on Mountain Dogs. Breeder/judge Mrs. Sylvia Howison's Best of Breed choice was again from Canada, Can. & Am. Ch. Alpenblick's Alpine Alpenwiede, CD, and her Best of Opposite Sex winner was Ch. De-Li's Chase the Clouds.

The Specialty in 1990 was held in May, with Oconomowoc, Wisconsin, hosting 346 Bernese Mountain Dogs and their owners. The judge was Mrs. James Edward Clark. This was also the year that began the judges study group to educate judges on the merits of the Bernese. This group had a worthy instructor in Mrs. Clark as she is very knowledgeable in many breeds! Mrs. Clarks' choice for Best of Breed was Ch. Heartlight's Baby Grand, and her Best of Opposite Sex winner was Ch. Fraulein Abigale De Miacis, CD. Mrs. Clark was unable to speak to the gathering about her choices, so the participants in the study group were asked to fill in. They al!

Ch. De-Li's Chase the Clouds (Bev's Black Jack v. BB ex Ch. Tonia v. Barenried), owned and bred by Lilian Ostermiller, was BOS at the 1989 BMDCA Specialty under breeder/judge Sylvia Howison. *Kohler*

commented on a need to improve fronts, particularly shoulders and toplines, as well as some houndy heads.

The 1991 Specialty was held in Coraopolis, Pennsylvania. There were 393 dogs in competition. The judge was from West Germany, the first foreign judge for a Specialty. His name was Christofer Habig and he presided over 324 dogs. Mr. Habig commented that the level of American Bernese Mountain Dogs was very high in soundness, movement and temperament, but that there were few straight shoulders, and fronts in general were not as good as hindquarters. He felt bodies were nicely balanced with very well angulated hindquarters. Heads should be strengthened as some stops were rather flat, some eyes light and some ears low set and pretty long. Mr. Habig chose an import, Ch. Donar v. Mutschen, for Best of Breed, and from the Veterans class, Ch. Shersan's Advanced Warning captured the Best of Opposite Sex trophy.

The 1992 Specialty was held in Colorado Springs, Colorado,

Ch. Heartlight's Baby Grand (Ch. Shersan's Chip Off the Ol' Block ex Ch. Heartlight's Autograph), owned and bred by Gail Vogel, was BB at the 1990 BMDCA Specialty.
Booth by Ritter

with the beautiful Rocky Mountains as a backdrop. The judge was Mr. Klaus Anselm, who chose Ch. Swiss Stars Blue Baron for Best of Breed, and Best of Opposite Sex went to Ch. Cita v. Sagispicher, an import. Baron comes down from the Shady Lady legacy. Cita was from the classes, and this was her second year in the Winners Bitch circle, having taken it from the puppy class the year before.

The 1993 Specialty was held in Kansas City, Missouri. The May weather was perfect and the lakeside setting was beautiful. There were 334 dogs in competition, and entries totaled 579. The judge, Dr. Quentin LaHam, well known for his movement seminars, did a very competent job. Dr. LaHam's choice for Best of Breed was from the 6 to 9 year Veterans class, and this was his second Best of Breed at a Specialty, Ch. Donar v. Mutschen, an import. Dr. LaHam commented that ''Donar or Alex'' was a true stallion

Ch. Fraulein Abigale De Miacis, CD (Ch. Shersan's Black Tie Required ex Mt. View's Mademoiselle Marie, CD), owned by Michael and Nancy Kepsel and bred by Dorothy Peters, was BOS at the 1990 Specialty. *Booth by Ritter*

of the breed. For Best of Opposite Sex, Dr. LaHam chose Ch. High Alps Jodi v. Bevs.

The 1994 Specialty was held in Carlisle, Pennsylvania, and the judges were Mr. and Mrs. John James from England. Mr. James judged the dog classes and intersex competition while Mrs. James presided over the bitches. This was the first BMDCA Specialty to run two rings at the same time, but the total entry of 875 made it necessary. Mr. James commented that he had eliminated all dogs with light eyes, as well as any he considered oversized or undersized, and he complimented North American breeders on their dogs' soundness and clean movement. He cautioned American breeders to import cautiously to avoid introducing unknown blemishes into the gene pool. For Best of Breed, Mr. James chose the American-bred Ch. De-Li's Foregone Conclusion and his Best of Opposite Sex choice was the Canadian-bred Ch. Arnika Vom Werdenfels.

Ch. Swiss Stars Blue Baron (Ch. Dallybeck's Echo Jackson ex Ch. Vonbreiterweg's Swiss Lace), owned by H. Michael and Karolyn Reed and bred by Bill and Bobbie Hefner, was BB at the 1992 BMDCA Specialty. *Warren Cook*

TOP PRODUCERS

The Bernese Mountain Dog Club of America honors sires and dams each year who produce a specified number of champion offspring. The number is different for dogs than it is for bitches, as a bitch can only produce so many litters in a lifetime and her breeding window is rather limited, usually from about two years to six or seven years. Dogs can continue to sire litters into old age without ill effects as it is not as stressful as whelping and rearing a litter. The number of offspring needed to qualify for this honor is six for a dog and four for a bitch. Every dog and bitch that qualify for this honor are indeed special, but some stand out as having gone well above and beyond the call of duty.

Ch. High Alps Jodi v. Bev's (Ch. Bev's Baron v. Greybern ex Bev's Latest Edition v. Jodi), owned by Angela Radel and bred by Beverly Burney, was BOS at the 1993 BMDCA Specialty. *Kohler*

The breed's all-time top-producing sire is Ch. Halidom Davos v. Yodlerhof, CD, OFA BMD-86. He sired more champions in both breed and obedience than any other dog in the history of the breed—he also won the Specialty! Proudly owned by Millicent Parliman, this great dog's breeder is James G. Brooks, Jr., of Greenwich, Connecticut. Happily, Jim's contributions to Bernese are long-term and far-reaching, for without him and his beloved Ch. Grand Yodler of Teton Valley, CDX, the breed would not have had Ch. Ashley v. Bernerliebe, CD, three-time Specialty Best of Breed winner (Ashley's dam was Davos's sister and Jim imported Ashley's sire, Galan) or Ch. Doska v. Yodlerhof, Specialty BOS winner. Credit for the biggest winning Bernese in history, Ch. Shersan Chang O'Pace v. Halidom, also goes to Jim Brooks, for it all started back with Ch. Grand Yodler of Teton Valley, CDX. ''Yodel'' was out of Ch. Hektor v. Nesselacker and Bella's Clara. His great-grandfather was Bobi v. Bauernheim, and one of his other great-

Ch. Donar v. Mutschen (Hansi B ex Assi B Mutschen), owned by Hans and JoDee Hauser and bred by Lotti Schrode, was BB at the 1991 and 1993 BMDCA Specialties, the latter from the Veterans' class. *Kohler*

grandfathers was CACIB Ch. Alex v. Bauernheim. Yodel was also the second Bernese in history to ever win a first in the Working Group in the United States.

Jim then made a few trips to Switzerland and returned with Ch. Ginger v. Senseboden and Ch. Galan v. Senseboden, who were both genetically doubled up on Ch. Alex v. Bauernheim in the fourth generation, as well as our Newfoundland cross boy, CACIB Alex v. Angstorf in the fifth. In fact Ginger and Galan were sired by Sultan v. Dursrutti, and the Dursrutti kennel was well known for its linebreedings on Alex.

Ginger sounded like a great combination with Yodel, and obviously she was! The Ohlsens and Buchanans took it from there!

Another breeder that stands out in this section is Mrs. Joe (Christine) Pike. Pikes kennel, located in Sequim, Washington, has bred more top producers than any other kennel in the history of the breed. Mrs. Pike began her breeding program with Ch. Bella's Cluny, bred by Harold Thompson out of Bella's Albertine and Arno v. d. Grasburg. Cluny was whelped November 18, 1968. Unfortu-

Ch. Grand Yodler of Teton Valley, CDX, owned by James G. Brooks, has had a far-reaching effect on the breed as a sire of great producers and significant winners.

nately the Pikes were unable to breed Cluny and soon added Ch. Bella's Albertine Faymie, also bred by the Thompsons, to their program.

Mrs. Pike also imported Christine v. d. Speichergasse, whose father, Bruno v. Bauernheim, was a brother to Bobi v. Bauernheim. Along with her mate, Ch. Edo v. Moosseedorf went back to CACIB Alex v. Bauernheim (same dam as Bobi and Bruno).

Christine v. d. Speichergasse and Ch. Edo v. Moosseedorf produced very well for the Pikes. Most notable was Ch. Pike's Siegfried v. Edo who became the number one Bernese for 1978 in breed points. He would have been the winner of today's Kal-Kan Pedigree Award.

The Pikes bred Siegfried to Ch. Bella's Albertine Faymie (once again a linebreeding on Bruno and Bobi v. Bauernheim) and produced the breeds' second Best in Show dog, Am. & Can. Ch. Pikes Harpo J. Andrew, owned by James Smalley. Siegfried was also bred to Faymie, producing Ch. Pike's Adonis v. Edo.

Am., Can. Ch. Arnika Vom Werdenfels (Ch. Dalleybeck's Echo Jackson ex Charlett von der Aub), owned by Deborah and Glenn Hotze and bred by Elke and Franz Hollenbach. Arnika was BOS at the 1994 Specialty under Mr. James. Mr. Hotze handled her to the win. *Tom DiGiacomo*

Adonis was bred to Christine v. d. Speichergasse and produced Ch. Darius of Rutherford, the breed's first Bermudian champion (once again a linebreeding on Bobi and Bruno). Darius managed to become a top producer of nine champions in his very short lifetime of two years.

The Pikes' top producers and their number of champion off-spring include Ch. Pike's Chewbacca, eighteen; Pike's Elsa v. Sieg-fried, thirteen; Ch. Pike's Bordeaux v. Languardo, nine; Ch. Darius of Rutherford, nine; Ch. Nova Polaris, eight; Ch. Pike's Siegfried v. Edo, six; Ch. Pike's Jewel v. Barenried, five; and Pike's Darla v. Edo, four.

Ch. De-Li's Foregone Conclusion (Ch. De-Li's Original Score ex Ch. De-Li's Foreign Intrigue), owned by John Dreaney and Lilian Ostermiller and co-bred by Mrs. Ostermiller and Cheryl Grau, is shown here winning the 1994 BMDCA Specialty under English judge John James. Michelle Ostermiller handled him to this coveted win.

Tom DiGiacomo

Top-Producing Bernese Mountain Dog Sires

Dog's Name	# Champions	Owner/Breeder
Ch. Halidom Davos v. Yodlerhof, CD	44	Millicent Buchanan Parliman/James G. Brooks, Jr.
Am., Can. Ch. Deer Park Heartlight	43	Denise Dean/Lisa Curtis & Denise Dean
Ch. De-Li's Foreign Touch	39	Lilian Ostermiller (breeder)
Am., Can. Ch. Shersan's Black Tie Required	35	Robert & Carolyn Kinley (breeders)

Dog's Name	# Champions	Owner/Breeder
Ch. Dallybeck's Echo Jackson	31	Marjorie & Andrew Reho (breeders)
Ch. Ashley v. Bernerliebe, CD	28	Joel & Christina Ohlsen (breeders)
Am., Can. Ch. Ch. Shersan Change O'Pace v. Halidom	26	Robert & Carolyn Kinley/Millicent Buchanan Parliman
Ch. Kuster's Jocko of J'Bar	24	G. Johnson & B. Kuster/ Alpstein Kennels
Am., Can. Ch. Jaycy's Wyatt Vom Hund See	23	Beverly Burney/Larry Rutter
Ch. Arthos October v. Berndach	23	Sharon C. Smith/Adele Miller & Richard Volpe
Ch. Ami VD Swiss Top Farm	21	W. & M. Townsend/V. Schaer
Ch. Majanco Languardo	21	Mrs. J. Pike/Mrs. Lendon-Ludwig
Ch. Alex von Weissenburg	20	Katherine Donohew/Herr Schofer (Switz.)
Ch. Broken Oaks Dieter v. Arjana, CD	19	Gale Werth (breeder)
Ch. De-Li's Standing Ovation	19	Lilian Ostermiller (breeder)

Top-Producing Bernese Mountain Dog Dams

Dog's Name	# Champions	Owner/Breeder
Ch. Trilogy's Title Role	18	Susan Tramp (breeder)
Ch. Shersan Bernhugel Hot Gossip	17	R. & C. Kinley & P. Dreisbach/Patricia Dreisbach
Ch. Texas Tiffany Vombreiterweg, CDX	16	S. Tramp/W. & M. Townsend

Dog's Name	# Champions	Owner/Breeder
Ch. Deer Park Ferkin v. Buttonwillow	15	Denise Dean/Diane Russ
Am., Can. Ch. Bev's Jabbering Jodi v. BB	14	Beverly Burney (breeder)
Ch. Sunnyhill's Anna v. Jimco	12	Sharon Kullman/James Cotter
Ch. Halidom Keri, CD	11	Millicent B. Parliman (breeder)
Am., Can., Bda. Ch. Alphorn's Happy Talk	10	B. Burney/D. & G. Johnson
Ch. Camelot's Hello Dolly	10	Art & Gwen Russel
Ch. Grundberg Iridescent Fire	10	Adele Miller & Richard Volpe/Deborah Mulvey
Pike's Elsa v. Siegfried	10	Mrs. Joe Pike (breeder)
Ch. Tonia v. Barenried	10	Lilian Ostermiller/Hans Jsch
Ch. Wyemede's Heidi Vombreiterweg	10	W. & M. Townsend/J. Crawford
Ch. Vombreiterweg's Swiss Lace	10	William & Barbara Hefner/ Walter & Mary Townsend
Ch. Windy Knob's Legacy DeGrasso	10	Barbara DeGrasso/Jerry Hughes

TOP CONFORMATION DOGS

Each year the Bernese Mountain Dog Club of America honors the top winning Group dogs, with one dog and one bitch chosen based on the largest number of points. These points are compiled by taking Group placements, Bests in Show and Best of Breed wins.

This proved particularly difficult before the Working Group/ Herding Group split in 1983.

BEST IN SHOW DOGS

The ultimate show honor is a "Best." To date (1994) only thirteen Bernese Mountain Dogs have won a Best in Show. I was extremely fortunate to have owned one, my beloved Ch. Arthos October v. Berndash, and to have bred one, Ch. October's A. Seekins. But this category has one true standout whose record remains the one to shoot for: Ch. Shersan Chang O'Pace v. Halidom with twenty Bests in Show. Pace's total points in Group and Bests one year reached over 14,000! Campaigning a dog at this level takes a lot of time and commitment. Those fortunate enough to have a relative in the family who is a professional handler are lucky indeed, for at least the expense is much less. This achievement requires a true commitment to the sport of dogs! A touch of insanity is another helpful ingredient.

Most, if not all, of these Best in Show Berners also go back

Am., Can. Ch. Pike's Harpo J. Andrew (Ch. Pike's Siegfried v. Edo ex Ch. Bella's Albertine Faymie), owned by James L. Smalley and bred by Christine Pike. "Harpo" was a multiple BIS dog, the top conformation dog from 1980 through 1983 and a sire of a number of noteworthy winners. *Lewis Roberts*

Am., Can. Ch. Shersan Change O'Pace v. Halidom (Ch. Halidom Davos v. Yodlerhof, CD, ex Ch. Halidom Kali v. Muensterplaz, CD), owned by Robert and Carolyn Kinley and bred by Millicent Buchanan Parliman. A highly successful show dog, "Pacer" had twenty BIS wins, BB at the 1986 Specialty, was the top conformation dog for 1984–86 and sired twenty-five champions. He was the first, and to date only, Bernese Mountain Dog to win the Working Group at the Westminster KC show. He is shown in this historic win in 1985 under judge Langdon L. Skarda.

John L. Ashbey

to those original dogs. Of course the first two Best in Show dogs, Ch. Alphorn's Copyright of Echo and Ch. Pike's Harpo J. Andrew are direct desendents. The third Best in Show dog, Ch. Shersan Chang O'Pace v. Halidom, was a linebreeding on Bella's Clara. The rest of the Best in Show dogs can also trace their heritage back to the relatives of those original dogs. Although I am uncertain about later imports, I doubt if traced back far enough that they could have escaped the influence of CACIB Alex v. Angstorf, Bruno v. Baurenheim or CACIB Zorro v. Muhlstein in their native land. CACIB Alex v. Angstorf surely helped the coats, since as late as 1922 there were reports of Bernese being exported from Switzerland with one parent who was listed in the Stud Book as "Red and White."

Bernese Mountain Dog Club of America
National Specialty Winners

Year	Dog	Owner/Breeder
1976	BOB Ch. Zyta v. Nesselacker (import)	Mary R. Dawson/Amadeus Krauchi
	BOS Ch. Goliath v. Zinggen	James Curtiss/C. Fankhauser
1977	BOB Ch. Alphorn's Copyright of Echo	Dr. & Mrs. D. G. Johnson (owner)
	BOS Ch. Car Mars A Miss v. Copyright, CD	Carolyn Lockhart (owner)
1978	BOB Ch. Alphorn's Copyright Of Echo	Dr. & Mrs. D. G. Johnson (owner)
	BOS Ch. Gina v. Zinggen	Esther Mueller/ C. Fankhauser
1979	BOB Ch. Halidom Davos v. Yodlerhof, CD	Millicent Buchanan-Parliman/James Brooks
	BOS Ch. Martha's Teddy Bear, CD, TD	Sam & Martha Decker/Floyd & Edna Paugh
1980	BOB Ch. Ashley v. Bernerliebe, CD	Christina & J. D. Ohlsen (owner)
	BOS Ch. Doska v. Yodlerhof	Mr. & Mrs. R. Ranck/James Brooks
1981	BOB Ch. Marens Ajax	Loyal & Lori Jodar/Marcus & Janice Ahrens
	BOS Ch. Broken Oaks Bergita, CD, TD	Andrew & Marjorie Reho/ Gale Werth
1982	BOB Ch. Ashley v. Bernerliebe, CD	Christina & J. D. Ohlsen (owner)
	BOS Tails N Hock Tasha of Black Mt.	Deborah Mulvey/Carol Lavell
1983	BOB Ch. Ashley v. Bernerliebe, CD	Christina & J. D. Ohlsen (owner)
	BOS Ch. Tauna's Lady Silvertip	Beverly Search/James Smalley
1984	BOB Ch. Broken Oaks Dieter v. Arjana	Gale Werth (owner)
	BOS Ch. Roundtops Abigail	Mary Jo & Mary Beth Thomson/William & Mary Jo Thomson
1985	BOB Bigpaws Yoda	Susan Quinn (owner)
	BOS Broken Oaks I-Ching	Gale Werth (owner)

Year	Dog	Owner/Breeder
1986	BOB Ch. Shersan Chang O'Pace v. Halidom, CD	Robert & Carolyn Kinley/ Millicent Buchanan
	BOS Gitana De Braye	Eve Menegoz/Willy Fawer
1987	BOB Ch. Harlaquin's Thor the Bear	Gina McDonnell/Kim Kilroy
	BOS Ch. Bornedale Puffin v. Ledgewood	Leon Kozikowski & Kim Behrens/Susan & Michael MacWilliams
1988	BOB Ch. DeerPark Heartlight	Denise Dean/Lisa Curtis & Denise Dean
	BOS Gitana De Braye	Eve Menegoz/Willy Fawer
1989	BOB Ch. Alpenblick's Alpine Alpenweide, CD	Philip & Dona Harness/Coral & David Denis
	BOS Ch. De-Li's Chase the Clouds	Lilian Ostermiller (owner)
1990	BOB Ch. Heartlight's Baby Grand	Gail Vogel (owner)
	BOS Ch. Fraulein Abigale De Miacis, CD	M. & N. Kepsel/Dorothy Peters
1991	BOB Ch. Donar v. Mutschen	Hans & Jo Dee Hauser & Edelweiss Vale/Lotti Schrode
	BOS Ch. Shersan's Advanced Warning	Robert & Carolyn Kinley (owner)
1992	BOB Ch. Swiss Stars Blue Baron	Michael & Karolyn Reed/ William & Barbara Hefner
	BOS Cita v. Sagispicher	Kim Behrens/Marianne Iff
1993	BOB Ch. Donar v. Mutschen	Hans & Jo Dee Hauser & Edelweiss Vale/Lotti Schrode
	BOS Ch. High Alps Jodi v. Bevs	Angela & David Radel/ Beverly Burney
1994	BOB Ch. De-Li's Foregone Conclusion	John Dreaney & Lilian Ostermiller/Cheryl Grau & Lilian Ostermiller
	BOS Ch. Arnika von Werdenfels	Deborah Hotze/Elke & Franz Hollenbach

Bernese Mountain Dog Club of America
Top Conformation Dog and Bitch

Year	Dog	Owner/Breeder
1976	BIS Ch. Alphorn's Copyright of Echo	Dr. & Mrs. D. G. Johnson (owner)
	Ch. Zyta v. Nesselacker (import)	Mary R. Dawson/Amadeus Krauchi
1977	BIS Ch. Alphorn's Copyright of Echo	Dr. & Mrs. D. G. Johnson (owner)
	Ch. Clara's Blass, CD	Marcus & Janice Aherns/ S. Howison & M. Decker
1978	BIS Ch. Alphorn's Copyright of Echo	Dr. & Mrs. D. G. Johnson (owner)
	Ch. Zyta v. Nesselacker (import)	Mary R. Dawson/Amadeus Krauchi
1979	Ch. Ashley v. Bernerliebe, CD	Joel & Christina Ohlsen (owner)
	Ch. Lady Rowena of Whitecross	Elizabeth Fuller/ Dr. Vernon C. Buckley
1980	BIS Am. & Can. Ch. Pike's Harpo J. Andrew	James L. Smalley/Mrs. Joe (Christine) Pike
	Ch. Vari's Land Cruiser Miss, CD	Bob & Vicki Groh/Carolyn Lockhart
1981	BIS Am. & Can. Ch. Pike's Harpo J. Andrew	Mr. James L. Smalley/Mrs. Joe (Christine) Pike
	Ch. Broken Oaks Bergita, CD, TD	Andrew & Marjorie Reho/ Gale Werth
1982	BIS Am. & Can. Ch. Pike's Harpo J. Andrew	James L. Smalley/Mrs. Joe (Christine) Pike
	Ch. Broken Oaks Bergita, CD, TD	Andrew & Marjorie Reho/ Gale Werth
1983	BIS Am. & Can. Ch. Pike's Harpo J. Andrew	James L. Smalley/Mrs. Joe (Christine) Pike
	Ch. Madchen von Barengragen	Leon & Harriet Gehorsam/ Edward & Pamela Lloyd
1984	BIS Ch. Shersan Chang O'Pace v. Halidom, CD	Robert & Carolyn Kinley/ Millicent Buchanan-Parliman
	Ch. Tauna's Lady Silvertip	Beverly Search/James L. Smalley

Ch. Madchen von Barengraben (Ch. Fels von Muensterplaz ex Roundtop's Kelli v. Engadine), owned by Leon and Harriet Gehorsam and bred by Edward and Pamela Lloyd, was the top conformation bitch for 1983 and produced four champions.

Stephen Klein

Bernese Mountain Dog Club of America
Top Conformation Dog and Bitch (*cont.*)

Year	Dog	Owner/Breeder
1985	BIS Ch. Shersan Chang O'Pace v. Halidom, CD	Robert & Carolyn Kinley/ Millicent Buchanan
	Am. & Can. Ch. Bigpaws Brigitta Alpenweide, CD	Philip & Donna Harness/ Susan Quinn/Forde
1986	BIS Ch. Shersan Chang O'Pace v. Halidom, CD	Robert & Carolyn Kinley/ Millicent Buchanan
	Ch. Jungfrau's Afternoon Delight	Gretchen Johnson/D. H. Harper

Ch. Jungfrau's Afternoon Delight (Can. Ch. Hasso vom Korschtal, CDX, ex Biggi von der Krummen Ebene), owned by Gretchen Johnson and bred by D.H. Harper, was the top conformation bitch of 1986. *Cott/Daigle/Francis*

Bernese Mountain Dog Club of America
Top Conformation Dog and Bitch (*cont.*)

Year	Dog	Owner/Breeder
1987	Am. & Can. Ch. DeerPark Heartlight	Denise Dean/Lisa Curtis & Denise Dean
	Ch. Bornedale Puffin v. Ledgewood	Leon Kozikowski & Kim Behrens/Susan & Michael MacWilliams
1988	BOB Ch. DeerPark Heartlight	Denise Dean/Lisa Curtis & Denise Dean
	Ch. Bornedale Puffin v. Ledgewood	Leon Kozikowski & Kim Behrens/Susan & Michael MacWilliams
1989	BIS Ch. Arthos October v. Berndach	Sharon C. Smith/Leon Kozikowski & Adele Miller & Richard Volpe

Ch. Deerpark Double Play, CD (Ch. Deerpark Heartlight ex Ch. Deerpark Ferkin v. Buttonwillow), owned by Joanne Prellberg and Dan Clay and bred by Denise Dean. A Working Group winner, she was the number one Bernese bitch for 1990.   *Cott*

Ch. Trilogy's Change O'Tempo (Ch. Shersan Change O'Pace v. Halidom, CD, ex Ch. Trilogy's Title Role), owned by Cindy Valentine and bred by Susan Tramp, was the number one Bernese bitch for 1991 and is the dam of six champions.   *Cott*

Bernese Mountain Dog Club of America
Top Conformation Dog and Bitch (*cont.*)

Year	Dog	Owner/Breeder
	Ch. De-Li's Chase the Clouds	Lilian Ostermiller (owner)
1990	BIS Ch. De-Li's Standing Ovation	Lilian Ostermiller (owner)
	Ch. DeerPark Double Play, CD	Joanne Prellberg & Dan Clay/Denise Dean
1991	BIS Ch. De-Li's Standing Ovation	Lilian Ostermiller (owner)
	Ch. Trilogy's Change 'O Tempo	Cindy Valentine/Susan Tramp
1992	BIS Ch. De-Li's Standing Ovation	Lilian Ostermiller (owner)
	Ch. Cita v. Sagispicher	Kim Behrens/Marianne Iff
1993	BIS Ch. De-Li's Foregone Conclusion	John Dreaney & Lilian Ostermiller
	Ch. De-Li's Trisha v. Nesselacker	Karen Desiderio/Lilian Ostermiller

3

Official Standard
of the Bernese
Mountain Dog

NO DISCUSSION OF the Standard would be complete without including previous versions so their evolution can be considered. The following is the original Standard as adopted in 1937 by the American Kennel Club for the Bernese Mountain Dog.

THE AKC STANDARD FROM 1937–1980

General appearance: A well-balanced dog, active and alert; a combination of sagacity, fidelity and utility.

Height: Dogs 23″ to 27½″; bitches 21″ to 26″ at the shoulder.

Head: Skull flat, defined stop and strong muzzle. Dewlaps very slightly developed, flews not too pendulous, jaw strong with good, strong teeth. Eyes dark, hazel brown, full of fire. Ears V-shaped,

The Bernese Mountain Dog has always been a stalwart, utilitarian animal, and the dog's conformation and attitude should make that abundantly clear to any observer. This typical male gives the unmistakable impression that he would be an invaluable asset to any Swiss dairy farm.

set on high, not too pointed at tips and rather short. When in repose, hanging close to head; when alert, brought slightly forward raised at base.

Body: Rather short than too long in back, compact and well ribbed up. Chest broad with good depth of brisket. Loins strong and muscular.

Legs and Feet: Forelegs perfectly straight and muscular, thighs well developed and stifles well bent. Feet round and compact. Dewclaws should be removed.

The typical female Bernese should appear just as useful and capable as a male, but she must also be distinctly feminine.

Tail: Of fair thickness and well covered with long hair, but not to form a flag; moderate length. When in repose, should be carried low, upward swirl permissible; when alert, may be carried gaily, but may never curl or be carried over the back.

Color and Markings: Jet black with russet brown or deep tan markings on all four legs, a spot just above forelegs, each side of white chest markings and spots over eyes, which may never be missing. The brown on the forelegs must always be between the black and white. Preferable, but not a condition, are: white feet, tip of tail, pure white blaze up the foreface, a few white hairs on the back of the neck and white star-shaped markings on the chest. When the latter markings are missing, it is not a disqualification.

Faults: Too massive in head, light or staring eyes, too heavy or long ears, too narrow or snipey muzzle, undershot or overshot mouth, pendulous dewlaps, too long or setterlike body, splay or hare feet, tail curled or carried over the back, cowhocks and white legs.

Scale of Points: General appearance—15; Size and Height—5; Head—15; Body—15; Legs and Feet—15; Tail—10; Coat—10; Color and Markings—15. Total—100.

This Standard was in use until 1980. The Bernese Mountain Dog Club of America appointed a committee to draft a new version that explained the qualities of these dogs more clearly, and much heated discussion flew back and forth with club members voicing their opinions on wording and faults that should be made a disqualification. The larger original committee was cut to a core group of Sylvia Howison and Esther Mueller with Mary Alice Horstick as clerk, at the request of Sylvia, who felt the original committee was too large (fifteen to twenty members).

Their original submission to the membership in 1977 contained the following disqualifications: Entropion, blue eye color and any color combination other than black, rust and white. After much discussion in the *Newsletter*, with the publishing of various points in the Standard, as well as an open forum at the Specialty, it was decided that the term ''rust'' was too vague for a breed with such a wide spectrum of tan to deep rust colors. Thus, the wording ''Tri-Color'' and the disqualification being any ground color other than black. Also, entropion was felt by some to be a medical problem like hip dysplasia, which a judge should not be asked to diagnose in the ring. This was a rather isolationist approach, as if judges were not commonly expected to pass judgment on this serious condition in many other breed Standards. The Bernese breed as a whole lost out on this one, as entropion would be almost wiped out today if it had been made a disqualification—the best laid plans of mice and men. Unfortunately, the problem is treated as any other fault, and many breeders continue to breed entropic dogs, producing puppies condemned to endure surgery in order to live a normal life.

The Standard that follows is the final draft approved by the AKC and was in use until 1990 when the Standard was again revised. This version was used as the basis for the first slide show to illustrate the breed Standard.

THE STANDARD FOR THE BERNESE MOUNTAIN DOG, ADOPTED AUGUST 1980 BY THE AMERICAN KENNEL CLUB

General Appearance: A sturdy, balanced, large, strong-boned dog. Intelligent and having an appearance of strength and agility suiting it to draft and droving work in mountainous regions. Dogs appear masculine, while bitches are distinctly feminine.

Head: Skull—flat and broad with a slight furrow and a well-defined but not exaggerated stop. Muzzle—strong and straight. Dry-mouthed. Teeth strong, scissors bite; complete dentition. Serious fault: overshot or undershot bite. Ears—medium-sized, triangular in shape, gently rounded at the tip, hanging close to the head when in repose, brought forward and raised at the base when alert. Eyes—dark brown, slightly oval in shape with close-fitting eyelids; expression intelligent, animated and gentle. Serious faults: inverted or everted eyelids. Disqualification: blue eye.

Neck and Body: Neck—strong and muscular and of medium length. Back—broad and firm. Topline level from withers to croup. Chest—deep and capacious with well-sprung ribs and brisket reaching at least to the elbows. Body—nearly square with overall body length measuring slightly greater than height at the withers. Loin—strong. Croup—broad and smoothly rounded to tail insertion.

Forequarters: Shoulders—moderately laid back, flat-lying, well muscled, never loose. Forelegs—straight and strong with the elbows well under the shoulders. Pasterns slightly sloping without weakness. Feet round and compact with well-arched toes. Dewclaws may be removed from front legs.

Hindquarters: Thighs—broad, strong and muscular. Stifles—moderately bent, tapering smoothly into hocks. Hocks—well let down and straight as viewed from the rear. Dewclaws should be removed from rear legs.

Tail: Bushy. Bone reaching to the hock joint or below. When in repose, tail should be carried low, upward swirl permissible when

65

alert. May be carried gaily, but may never curl or be carried over the back. Fault: kink in tail.

Coat: Thick, moderately long, slightly wavy or straight, with a bright natural sheen.

Color and Markings: Tri-color—jet black ground color with rich rust and clear white markings. Markings (symmetry desired)—Rust: over each eye; on cheeks, preferably reaching at least to the corner of the mouth; on each side of chest; on all four legs; under tail. White: blaze and muzzle band; chest marking, typically forming an inverted cross; feet; tip of tail. Faults: markings other than as described to be faulted in direct relationship to the extent of the deviation. Serious Faults: white legs; white collars. Disqualifications: any ground color other than black.

Gait: Natural working gait is a slow trot, but capable of speed and agility in keeping with use in draft and droving work. Good reach in front. Powerful drive from the rear transmitted through a level back. No wasted action. Front and hind legs on each side follow through in the same plane. At increased speed, legs tend to converge toward the center line.

Height: Dogs—24½″ to 27½″ at the withers. Bitches—22½″ to 25½″ at the withers.

Temperament: Self-confident, alert and good-natured. Never sharp or shy. A dog which will not stand for examination shall be dismissed from the ring.

Disqualifications: Blue eye color. Any ground color other than black.

The following Standard is a slight modification of the 1980 version, requested by the AKC to bring all Standards into the same format. This was an opportunity to further clarify some vague areas, such as foot markings and just how far up the leg should they go.

STANDARD FOR THE BERNESE MOUNTAIN DOG, ADOPTED MARCH 28, 1990, BY THE AMERICAN KENNEL CLUB

General Appearance: The Bernese Mountain Dog is a striking, tri-colored, large dog. He is sturdy and balanced. He is intelligent, strong and agile enough to do the draft and droving work for which he was used in the mountainous regions of his origin. Dogs appear masculine, while bitches are distinctly feminine.

Size, Proportion, Substance: Measured at the withers, dogs are 25 to 27½ inches; bitches are 23 to 26 inches. Though appearing square, Bernese Mountain Dogs are slightly longer in body than they are tall. Sturdy bone is of great importance. The body is full.

Head: *Expression* is intelligent, animated and gentle. The *eyes* are dark brown and slightly oval in shape with close-fitting eyelids. Inverted or everted eyelids are serious faults. Blue eye color is a disqualification. The *ears* are medium-sized, set high, triangular in shape, gently rounded at the tip, and hang close to the head when in repose. When the Bernese Mountain Dog is alert, the ears are brought forward and raised at the base; the top of the ear is level with the top of the skull. The *skull* is flat on top and broad, with a slight furrow and a well-defined but not exaggerated stop. The *muzzle* is strong and straight. The *nose* is always black. The *lips* are clean, and as the Bernese Mountain Dog is a dry-mouthed breed, the flews are only slightly developed. The *teeth* meet in a scissors bite. An overshot or undershot bite is a serious fault. Dentition is complete.

Neck, Topline, Body: The *neck* is strong, muscular and of medium length. The *topline* is level from the withers to the croup. The *chest* is deep and capacious with well-sprung, but not barrel-shaped, ribs and brisket reaching at least to the elbows. The back is broad and firm. The *loin* is strong. The *croup* is broad and smoothly rounded to the tail insertion. The tail is bushy. It should be carried low when in repose. An upward swirl is permissible when the dog is alert, but the tail may never curl or be carried over the back. The bones in the tail should feel straight and should reach to the hock joint or below. A kink in the tail is a fault.

Forequarters: The shoulders are moderately laid back, flat-lying, well muscled and never loose. The legs are straight and strong and the elbows are well under the shoulder when the dog is standing. The *pasterns* slope very slightly, but are never weak. Dewclaws may be removed. The *feet* are round and compact with well-arched toes.

Hindquarters: The *thighs* are broad, strong and muscular. The *stifles* are moderately bent and taper smoothly into the hocks. The *hocks* are well let down and straight as viewed from the rear. *Dewclaws* should be removed. Feet are compact and turn neither in nor out.

Coat: The *coat* is thick, moderately long and slightly wavy or straight. It has a bright natural sheen. Extremely curly or extremely dull-looking coats are undesirable. The Bernese Mountain Dog is shown in natural coat and undue trimming is to be discouraged.

Color and Markings: The Bernese Mountain Dog is tri-colored. The ground color is jet black. The markings are rich rust and clear white. Symmetry of markings is desired. Rust appears over each eye, on the cheeks reaching to at least the corner of the mouth, on each side of the chest, on all four legs and under the tail. There is a white blaze and muzzle band. A white marking on the chest typically forms an inverted cross. The tip of the tail is white. White on the feet is desired but must not extend higher than the pasterns. Markings other than described are to be faulted in direct relationship to the extent of the deviation. White legs or a white collar are serious faults. Any ground color other than black is a disqualification.

Gait: The natural working gait of the Bernese Mountain Dog is a slow trot. However, in keeping with his use in draft and droving work, he is capable of speed and agility. There is a good reach in front. Powerful drive from the rear is transmitted through a level back. There is no wasted action. Front and rear legs on each side follow through in the same plane. At increased speed, legs tend to converge toward the center line.

Temperament: The temperament is self-confident, alert and good-natured, never sharp or shy. The Bernese Mountain Dog should stand steady, though may remain aloof to the attentions of strangers.

Disqualifications: Blue eye color. Any ground color other than black.

These three Standards demonstrate the evolution of the Bernese Mountain Dog in America, from a rather loose beginning when white markings were not neccassary to the current Standard that calls for clear white and limits its boundaries! This breed has come a long way since the early beginnings of the BMDCA, which has done much to promote this wise, loyal and useful breed. My only disappointment with the current Standard is that the three words originally used to describe the Bernese and that so aptly suit this breed are missing—sagacity, fidelity and utility.

In the fall of 1992 a video was filmed in New Jersey to illustrate the new Standard. Dogs from all over the United States were invited to participate in this production presided over by the American Kennel Club and the BMDCA. The taping committee consisted of breeder-judge Karen Ward; Debbie Mulvey, BMDCA past president; Lori Jordar, BMDCA past president, and Mr. J. D. Jones, AKC licensed Working Group judge. Unfortunately it rained for the entire day, but the resulting tape is a valuable educational tool for breeder, judge and fancier alike. The video can be ordered directly from AKC or from many dog show supply mail-order catalogs.

WHAT IS TYPE?

The differences that set one breed apart from another are considered typical for that breed. A Bernese is typically a sturdy farm dog used for draft and droving work as well as a watchdog and companion. His markings are striking and his appearance commanding, befitting that of a guard dog. Anyone approaching a farm with a typical Bernese barking a loud throaty warning would think twice before continuing without the approval of this impressive beast's owner. A long, beautiful coat and sturdy bone complete the picture of this animal whose origins are clearly those of fields and mountains.

He is harmonious in every way; nothing is exaggerated. He is a natural, well-balanced dog.

Many people will accept an unsound animal that moves wide

This group of Bernese siblings and their dam (third from left) makes an interesting study in correct breed type and consistency within a family group.

in the front, crosses over in the rear and has little or no neck if it has breed type. Others would prefer a dog that is clean coming and going with correct length of neck and proper movement even if it lacks breed type. I believe this is heavily influenced by what breeders have in their backyards as opposed to what they want in their backyards. I doubt if there is a breeder alive who wouldn't rather have both soundness and type if given a magic wand with which to create the ideal Bernese Mountain Dog. Short of genetic engineering, breeders are limited to what they have for breeding stock, thus the pull. I for one believe that a dog that combines both type and soundness should be the goal and that one component without the other is diminished in quality. The Bernese is a dog with all qualities in moderation, as the breed was intended to be—not tall, oversized 29-inch males or small, undersized 21-inch bitches.

Of course no discussion of type would be complete without covering those features not typical of the breed. These are often the very features that make a dog unable to perform his normal duties.

Atypical of the Bernese Mountain Dog

Open elegance and beauty that no longer gives a strong farm hand look is wrong for a Bernese. A racy salon dog appearance more befitting a sporting animal or racing animal is also undesirable. Bernese agility is that befitting droving, not a race course.

Bernese were not used for open herding like herding dogs but more for prodding cows along with their noses. If the cows became extremely difficult to manage the dogs would grab them by the nostrils to enforce their authority.

A slender animal not suited to draft work would not describe a Bernese. Consider trying to use thoroughbred horses to pull the Anheuser-Busch beer wagon and you've got the picture. Now reconsider the same wagon pulled by the traditional Anheuser-Busch Clydesdales (who always remind me of Bernese in their markings) and you have the true picture of a sturdy, well-balanced animal. Good Bernese are very much like a Clydesdales, for in spite of their bulk, their movement should be effortless.

TEMPERAMENT AND CHARACTERISTICS

My favorite phone call always starts, "Do you breed Bernese Mountain Dogs? I want one, can you tell me about the breed?" My first thought is always, "Why do you want one if you know nothing about the breed?"

Then my kinder instincts kick in and I'm transported back in time to the first time I saw a Bernese Mountain Dog and thought, "What is that lovely creature?" They are so beautiful and what markings! Add the appeal of the shiny coat and engaging expression—of course people want one! Who wouldn't!

But those engaging looks are only the surface. Berners have engaging temperaments to boot. This breed is completely devoted to their families or owners. The best description and one well deserved is, "Where do you find a Bernese Mountain Dog? On your foot!"

Bernese like to keep in touch. So just to make sure you are with them, they have a habit of backing up and sitting on their owners' feet. As puppies they are outgoing and love everyone. As adults they become more selective and are aloof to strangers, although, given time, they warm up. They prefer to be given comfortable space until they have sized up a new acquaintance. Once they become friendly, they usually remember who they've met before and will welcome their new acquaintance on successive visits.

Then there is the "Berner Bump." This involves a Bernese sticking its head under your hand or arm and forcefully nudging it until you provide the petting, with no regard for full coffee cups, telephone receivers or what ever else. Perhaps this is a holdover from their farm days spent poking the cows!

Bernese also feel that they are lifelong puppies and should still fit in your lap at ninety pounds. This habit can be subdued, but keep a wary eye for an occasional flying leap into your lap when you're not looking and most vulnerable.

They are dedicated to their families and adapt to any living situation. In the city, they learn to meet and greet all; in the country, they protect their homes just as their ancestors did. Bernese make wonderful, dependable watchdogs who sound ferocious, but usually aren't.

Because of their size, they do require daily exercise. Bernese usually stay close to home and come when they are called, with one exception. Some seem to pass through a phase between six and eighteen months when they run the other way and look at you as if you had two heads. This does pass, but a leash is the only way to make it through this period with your puppy intact. This phase usually corresponds with a hormonal surge—call it teen rebellion.

They are very intelligent and easy to train. Bernese pups readily fall into their new owner's routine and adapt very well. Some are more willful than others, and some are more active than others. But most make wonderful, devoted family dogs.

Sagacity equals wisdom, fidelity equals loyalty, utility equals usefulness—these are the key words to the Bernese temperament. Also, they are without cunning.

In the nineteenth century, Dr. Scheidegger gave this wonderful accounting of Bernese character as related by Dr. Albert Heim.

> The correct Bernese Mountain Dog is perfect for the Swiss farmer in character as is no other breed. According to a farmer, a dog is good if he is alert and keen without biting, follows at heel when walking, walks between the back wheels of a wagon, does not run in freshly cultivated fields, defends his master in need, watches tools left in the fields, is not wild, leaves cats and chickens alone, does not wander around. In mountainous regions the character of guarding and heading cattle is valued, whereas in the lowlands it is the aptitude for draft service. It is noteworthy that many Sennenhunde do all these tasks without special training.
>
> The vigilance especially is a strongly prominent trait, as well as

heeling with the masters, which many do completely from their own motives to duty. Whenever a Bernese Mountain Dog does not do one or another of these things by itself, it is usually easy to train to do them. However, if one requires other things that are not in his centuries-old duties, such as police dog tasks, water and hunting dog work, usually all these efforts fail with an open aversion and lack of understanding by the dog.

How can one explain these natural constant talents of the Bernese Mountain Dog, especially for the purposes of agriculturists? Without doubt it arises from the fact that the Bernese has been kept for centuries by country people, and again and again these same characteristics have been required and cultivated in them, and that for breeding the best in these working characters have been used most, so that finally these have become inherited features of this breed.

The past, the surroundings from which the Sennenhunde stem, is also recognizable in their behavior. Thus, they are rural in character and generally do not possess fine manners by themselves. From this it does not necessarily follow that they cannot be trained during their youth, as other dogs. But being obedient is often forgotten. The Sennenhunde is often a free daredevil who exercises his good qualities also with a certain storminess. Luckily at a certain age these dogs become quieter and reasonable, and very many become just as one likes them. The current saying about Bernese has become: Three years a young dog, three years a good dog, three years an old dog.

A dog is what men have made of him. One recognizes in his possible faults more the faults of his master than inborn vices of the pupil. A Bernese Mountain Dog with which his master gives much learns many things through his intelligence and friendliness that were not included in the old farm experience. Good Bernese Mountain Dogs attach themselves to schoolchildren as the truest playmates and then learn retrieving, basket carrying and many things that are not inborn. They are very alert observing everything, give evidence of the highest intelligence and, like all Sennenhunde, are without any cunning. They are keen and fearless but are not brawlers. These are all prevailing, sought-after breed characteristics.

Like the Appenzeller and the Entlebucher, the Bernese Mountain Dog finds lost cattle, drives them to the milking place, takes care of their arrangement and drives them on the street. In doing this the Bernese Mountain Dog, like the Appenzeller, pushes on the cattle as much as possible only with the muzzle, without biting. In cases of disobedience by the cattle, he does not seize in the convenient height, as does the quicker, smaller Appenzeller, which is evasive

"The Berner hug" demonstrated here and described in the text is every bit as typical of the breed as its size and unique color pattern.

after the nip, but quite low at the feet so that the kick of the cow goes over the dog into the air. When necessary the Bernese Mountain Dog grasps the cattle by the nostrils.

The Sennenhunde character is shown quite especially in the Berner by the breed's easy keeping. They take everything contentedly. They eat quickly in their particular way. They are very weather-resistant, tough and durable. Thanks to their medium-size, their weather-resistance, their few demands for activity, their particular self-training

"The Berner smile."

and their excellent house dog characters as well as their beauty, they are called more and more to become the national house and companion dog and to displace the foreign breeds, as long as one demands no police dog training or hunting dog characteristics of a dog. It is an effective duty of the breeders on the one hand to preserve the many good characters of the Bernese and on the other to cultivate not only their outer form and color but also their behavior.

I hear many stories of these characteristics today. One breeder commented to me that whenever she had a female in for breeding, one of her males would bop her with his nose to get her to respond to him, much as the early Bernese herded cattle by pushing with the muzzle. Most Bernese achieve their goals in much the same manner.

One of my puppies heels directly behind my feet no matter where I go—and I can't help thinking of a farm dog walking behind the wheels of a wagon.

A few are accomplished at the Bernese hug! This is a special habit of wrapping the front legs around your leg and holding on. This habit can endear people to the breed as no other—except possibly the smile—many Bernese grin from ear to ear.

TEETH ALIGNMENT AND BITES

This can be a very frustrating area in Bernese as they often have a different scissors bite from that of, say, a Sporting dog. Many lovely Bernese have this bite as shown in Figure 1 and Photo A. Figure 1 shows a scissors bite with right and left bottom incisors (slightly) forward (A and B). This is the typical Bernese scissors bite and is not undershot as some judges believe. Photo B shows a true scissors bite (rarely seen in a Bernese), and Figure 3 and Photo C shows a level bite also acceptable in a Bernese. Figures 4, 5 and 6 are all untypical bites and are serious faults.

Let's start with Figure 5, Photo D. This is called undershot because the bottom (or under) incisors are shot forward. This bite is an actual jaw misalignment causing all of the molars to become misaligned and can ruin the look of the head, as in Photo E. The dog on the right in this photo is undershot. Figure 4 is the reverse. The top incisors overshoot the bottom—causing all the same prob-

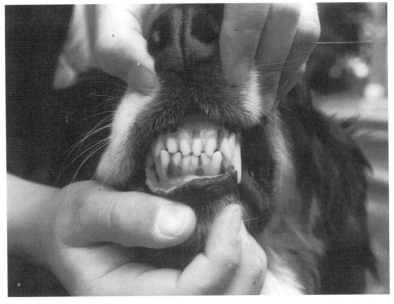

A

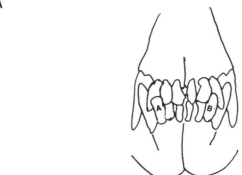

Fig. 1. Normal scissors bite. In Bernese, misaligned incisors A and B are quite common.

lems. But remember, these are problems in the show ring; these bites do not keep a dog from leading a normal life and being a wonderful pet, but they do eliminate its use as a breeding animal.

Lastly, we have the wry bite—people often can't decide about this one. Scissors or not, if your dog's bite is uneven and has a gaping hole, it's wry or crooked. Webster defines wry as ''having a bent or twisted shape or condition (a wry smile esp.: turned abnormally to one side).'' This bite is extremely faulty and should

76

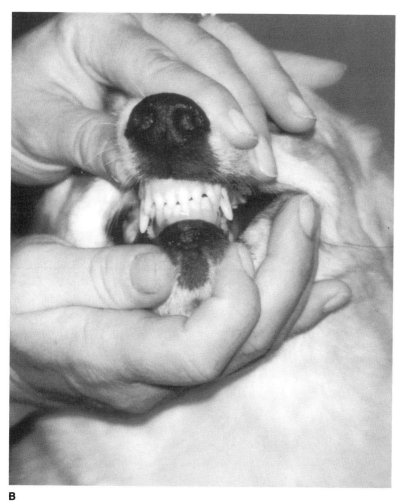

B

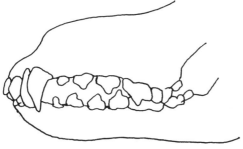

Fig. 2. The preferred scissors bite

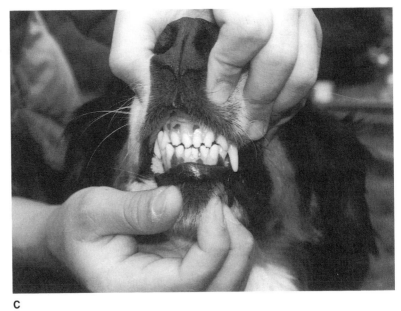

c

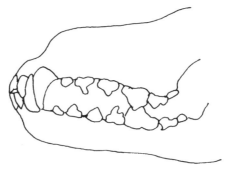

Fig. 3. The level bite is acceptable and is *not* considered a fault.

78

Bite Faults

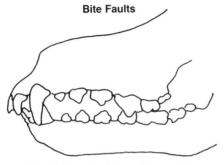

Fig. 4. Overshot bite or "Parrot Mouth"

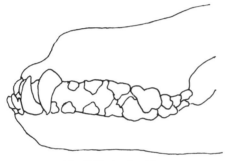

Fig. 5. Undershot bite

D

79

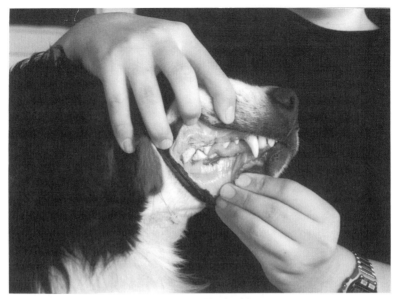

E   Incomplete side dentition

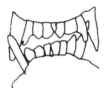

Fig. 6. "Wry Mouth"

never be used in a breeding program. Bernese should have complete dentition. Missing molars are faults.

HEAD AND EXPRESSION

A good head is essential to a correct Bernese Mountain Dog. There is nothing more disturbing than observing a lovely body combined with a head only a mother could love. Setter or Collie-like heads diminish true type, as do overdone Saint Bernard–type heads.

These extreme differences are easily spotted. The subtler differences are harder to recognize. You may sense that something is not quite right, but not know exactly what.

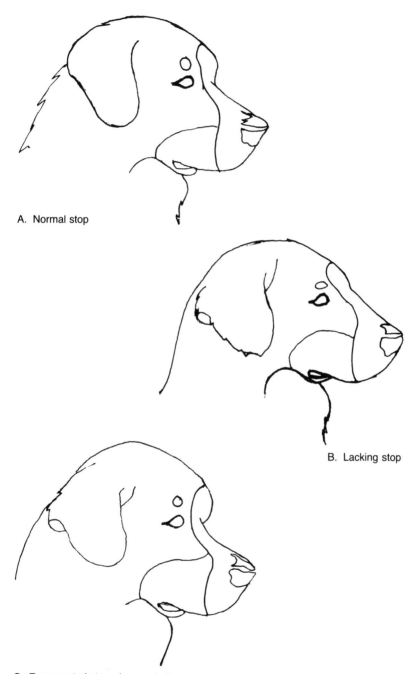

A. Normal stop

B. Lacking stop

C. Exaggerated stop, domey skull

Fig. 7. **Stop**

81

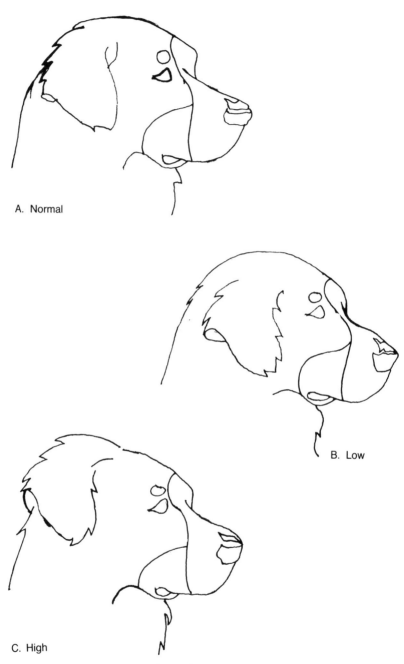

A. Normal

B. Low

C. High

Fig. 8. **Alert Ear Set**

82

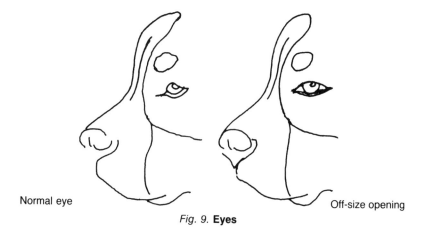

Normal eye Off-size opening

Fig. 9. **Eyes**

Figure 8 shows the same head again with three different ear sets. A shows a normal, alert ear set, B shows the same head with a low ear set, giving a houndy, rather common look to an otherwise pleasing head. C shows a high ear set, making an otherwise acceptable head look puppyish and unfinished.

Other distractions include round, bulging goldfish eyes, light yellowish bird of prey eyes and overdeveloped, pendulous flews that cause drooling, ruling out the dry-mouthed requirement. One or more of these traits in combination can turn a Bernese head into a caricature.

Lately I have noticed a new twist, a very odd eye. The socket appears to have been created too large for the eyeball. This is not an ectropic eye but rather an eye with too much room to the right and left of the eyeball, as in Figure 9. The haw is exposed in the corners. This results in a blank look and a dull expression, instead of the "fire-behind-the-eyes" look of intelligence. Sagacity is an important part of expression.

TAILSET AND CARRIAGE

Tailset is just what it sounds like, the set on, or attachment of, the tail to the spine. A tail that seems to pop up out of the back before the rump is set too high and a tail that comes from somewhere below the rounding of the croup is set too low.

High tail set

Low tail set

Normal position in repose

Fig. 10. **Tail Sets**

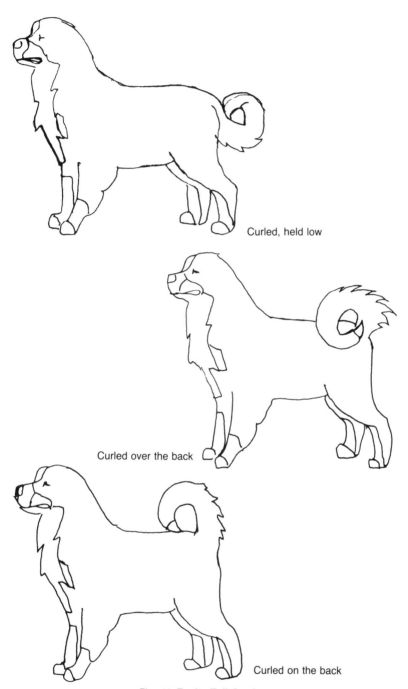

Curled, held low

Curled over the back

Curled on the back

Fig. 11. **Faulty Tail Carriages**

All these are examples of unacceptable tail carriage for the Bernese Mountain Dog.

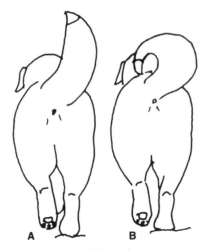

Fig. 11A.

A. The tail may be slightly gay when the dog is alertly moving.
B. When the dog is moving, the tail should never curl or be held over the back.

Tail carriage is closely related to tailset, but may be influenced by other factors such as curls or kinks. A normal tailset can be completely altered by a tail that rolls up into a tight, doughnut curl even if it isn't carried over the back. A kink sometimes causes a tail to take a sudden 90-degree turn (often called a wry tail). These are very distracting faults, but not as distracting as a curl carried over the back resembling the tail of an Akita or a Samoyed. This tail carriage makes the dog look unbalanced, too short in back and untypical for the breed.

Tail kinks are not always visible and can often only be found by running a hand down the length of the tail, feeling the bones. Careful examination in this manner will help find these bumps or kinks in the bones of the tail.

Proper tail carriage allows for an upward swirl, particularly in male dogs when they are alert and full of themselves when moving. In Figure 12 a slight bend at the end of this swirl should not be confused with an actual curl or kink.

Tail length is very important. The tail should reach at least to the hock or below. This can be measured by pulling the end of the tail between the back legs toward the ground while the dog is standing. The bones at the end of the tail, not the hair, should reach at least to the hock joint or below. Bernese are sometimes born with an extremely short tail, often as short as four to six inches at matu-

86

Fig. 12. **Correct Tail Carriage**
The three tail carriages illustrated here are all acceptable to the breed Standard.

rity. This is a mutation and although Berners so affected make fine pets, they should not be used in a breeding program.

COAT TEXTURE, COLOR AND MARKINGS

Bernese puppies start out with thick, fuzzy coats and not much length. At four to six months of age they begin to shed these baby coats and often put on a wavy or even curly coat (particularly near the spine). After adolescence they shed this puppy coat and finally develop an adult coat; this entire process can take up to two years to complete. Any one or all of these sheds can cause the coat to turn dull and develop a reddish cast as the old coat dies and the new coat pushes through. This is a good time to keep your dog out of the ring until the changeover is complete.

When all is said and done the coat should end up black, shiny and either wavy or flat. There are still many Bernese with rather curly coats and many of these are champions. The Standard does say extremely curly or extremely dull is undesirable. This leaves much room for interpretation and one person's extreme may not be as severe as another's. The best determiner is function. If the coat is so tightly curled that it retains snow and water and the dog dries very slowly, then the coat is too curly and therefore undesirable. A dull coat always appears dirty and dusty and simply does not clean well, as it lacks the proper oils often because of poor nutrition. This is also an undesirable coat as it retains burrs, twigs and other natural debris.

The Bernese has a very functional double coat, consisting of a softer undercoat that serves as an insulating layer against extreme temperatures (much like duck or goose down) and a longer, rougher outercoat. In the spring the undercoat is usually shed, leaving a slightly racier dog behind.

The ground color is black. There have been a few rare cases of bi-color Bernese, usually tan or rust with typical Bernese white markings and dark brown pigment.

I once saw an adult bi-color named ''Dusty'' (Bauernhof's Beau Jeste) at a Specialty in Wisconsin. Dusty's parents were tri-color Bernese and all but two of his littermates were also tri-color Bernese. Dusty and his red-and-white littermates are throwbacks to

During the second half of the 1970s, four litters were born in the United States that were reported to include red and white puppies out of normal, tri-colored parents. Two of these were mother/son breedings while a third was a half-brother/half-sister mating through a common dam—Shamrock's Molly McGuire. All three litters had four common ancestors in the fifth generation—Arno v.d. Grasburg, his dam Rita v.d. Grasburg, Bella's Albertine and Bobi v. Bauernheim. The earliest litter also went back to these dogs but was from a half-brother/half-sister mating with Arno as sire of both and Albertine as the dam of one. This breeding also doubles on Rita and Bobi in the third generation.

Susan Shambeau, breeder of the three later litters, kept a puppy from each and later bred red and white individuals together. Two of these, "Dusty" and "Heidi," produced an entire litter of these bi-colors and, in so doing, established the recessive nature of the color phase. Here "Dusty" and three tri-color kennel mates provide an interesting color contrast between what is familiar and what is not.

original farm dogs. Many of the early "red-and-white" Bernese were exported as St. Bernards when Saints were becoming popular. The following quote by Dr. Albert Heim, made just after the turn of the century, makes color priorities clear: "We want to establish black with the red and white markings, excluding dogs without black as undesirable peculiarities. The entirely yellow or red-yellow will become more and more rare." Undoubtedly, the yellow he is referring to is probably what we now call tan or cream. This would lead one to believe that these bi-colors once occurred commonly enough to be discussed openly, and indeed they have become rare.

In the Bernese, facial markings are of considerable importance to the integrity of type. In the examples shown on these two pages, Figs. 1 through 5 are all in the acceptable range with Figs. 2 and 3 being considered the most ideal. Figs. 1 and 6 are extremes with Figs. 6 through 8 being considered outside the ideal.

5

6

7

8

Markings are important, as the Bernese is a marked breed and total lack of attention to such things would destroy the striking coloration typical of this majestic canine. But there are many allowable variations that add interest to the faces and overall look.

Remember, the 1937 Standard called for a few white hairs on the back of the neck. Recently a noted judge confided that she could not consider the best specimen in the ring because it had a few white hairs on the back of the neck. I found this amazing as I had observed the judging, and this same judge had awarded the points to a dog with white extending beyond the lip on the judges side and lacking rust on the same side. My point is that the best dog should be awarded the points, even if it has a slight marking deviation. Judges that set themselves up to have to eliminate dogs from their consideration on the basis of slight marking deviations will find themselves doing a poor job of adjudicating. Small imperfections should be treated as such; markings are important, but must be kept in perspective as part of the overall picture and not be treated as disqualifications. To not consider a dog with a slightly asymmetrical muzzle band, a cross lacking rust on one side or no tail tip is to, in effect, disqualify that dog on that day. Judges who seize on such points instead of judging positively do not deserve an entry. Don't get me wrong. I'm not advocating that dogs with white collars and legs or high socks should be champions, but that minor imperfections be treated as such. Again, if we go back to that old 1937 Standard, when a scale of points was assigned, markings were 15 percent of the total dog or 15 points, so a faulty tail tip can matter but little. Seems like much ado over nothing. I have observed many judges digging through ends of tails for white hairs making fools of themselves, while missing much larger but harder-to-spot deviations.

OVERALL CONFORMATION

When you evaluate a Bernese, look for a dog with a level topline whose action is transmitted through a level back (doesn't bounce up and down in the rear) with good length of neck (avoid dogs that lack neck as this usually goes hand and hand with a lack of shoulder angulation and poor overall balance). Look for a dog that appears to almost float or not touch the ground as it moves.

This is effortless movement and usually indicates a sound dog. This should be combined with a look that is pleasing to the eye, nothing out of place, good bone and a healthy shiny coat of moderate length. Side movement should exhibit good reach in front (no hackney fronts that lift rather than reach—high steppers waste action) and good drive from the rear (high rear kickers also waste action and are usually compensating for a poor front).

To enable you to decide at ringside why one dog moves better than another, there must be a vocabulary. I've already described some things that are essential to a good-moving dog but they may mean nothing to you. I will now attempt to give you some of this vocabulary through a visual dictionary—drawings of the correct and incorrect as well as photos to help you interpret what you see. Hopefully this will help with stud selection, puppy selection and overall knowledge of the breed in general.

ANGULATION AND PROPORTIONS

Angulation is a necessary ingredient in the appearance and working ability of the Bernese Mountain Dog. Proper angulation and balance allow a dog to move freely. The angles of the bones in the shoulder and hip joints are the ones commonly referred to when discussing angulation. Many people are in doubt about where these angles occur and often confuse turn of the rear stifle with angulation. These two joints act as shock absorbers taking the impact from the ground. This operates best when the shoulder blade and upper arm in the front are of equal length and when the pelvis and hip bone are of the same length. This gives the dog balance front and rear and allows for reach and drive. The set-on of the front is also important, for if it is too far forward there will be an absence of sternum or forechest, and if it is set too far back there will be a preponderance of forechest. Either way, this is not desirable in a Bernese, which does indeed need a moderate amount of forechest on which to rest the breastplate of the harness and not have it interfere with the movement of the shoulders. Angulation is a necessary part of function, and since a Bernese is a draft dog, moderate angulation is preferred. Most important is balance—the angle in front should match that of the rear.

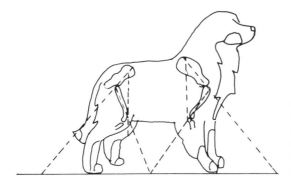

Fig. 13. A well-balanced structure with equal length of humerus and femur, correct angulation front and rear, harmonious and moderate throughout.

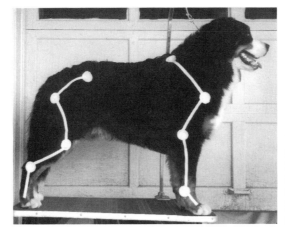

This "living schematic" shows the location of the bones in the front and rear assembly of this well-balanced, correctly angulated Bernese.

Fig. 14. This structure lacks both front and rear angulation evidenced by the abrupt junction of the neck to the withers, longcast impression and overall cloddy look. Interestingly, this structure has the same height and bone as the example in Fig. 13.

94

Pasterns can be an indication of good angulation as well as poor. Strong carpal joints and pasterns with a slight bend cushion the impact with the ground when a dog is moving. The proper pastern is strong and straight to the carpal joint, or knee, and from the knee to the foot there is a slight bend that adds springiness to the step. This type of pastern goes hand and hand with a well-angulated front. A dog that lacks front angulation will often "knuckle over." Knuckling over is just that, the carpal joint is thrust forward by too steeply set shoulders and the dog's forelegs appear to be over his pasterns. This should not be confused with the large bone development in the carpal joints of a large-boned growing dog. Picture a gorilla using its knuckles to support itself in the front as it walks and you have the idea.

Dogs can also "knuckle over" in the rear because of hyperextention of the hock; this is often referred to as straight stifles. This is caused by obtuse rear angulation.

Not all dogs are balanced; many unbalanced dogs are deceiving when standing still but usually give their faults away when moving.

Proportions may or may not be related to angulation. A dog may have correct angulation and just be long on back, or may have correct angulation and be too long in leg.

FRONTS

Standing

The way a dog stands freely on its own often betrays the movement to be displayed. The correct front stance is front legs parallel with toes just slightly off center for balance.

When this type of front moves, the dog, to achieve balance, will angle its legs inward toward a center line under its body. As speed increases the dog will begin to single track (put one foot down in a straight line in front of another).

Again, when a dog stands freely on its own many faults become visible that careful manipulation can often hide in the show ring. The photos on pp. 99–100 demonstrate faulty fronts.

"Toeing out" or "east-west" fronts are common in young dogs trying to achieve balance, but they are only acceptable in

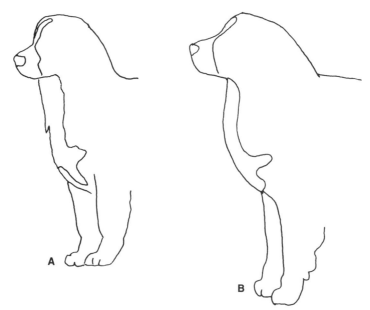

Fig. 15. A proper bend of pastern (A) is strong and is in keeping with a well-angulated front. With correct front angulation the neck will blend smoothly into the withers. By contrast the pasterns of dog B are "knuckling over" due to an upright shoulder. Compare the abrupt junction of neck and shoulder in the two drawings.

It is also possible for a dog to knuckle over in the rear legs due to hyperextension of the hocks. Often referred to as straight stifles, the condition is due to obtuse rear angulation. Such dogs are often overly angulated in front, so appear to go "downhill" when they move.

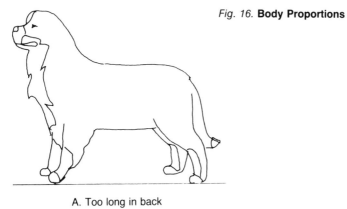

Fig. 16. **Body Proportions**

A. Too long in back

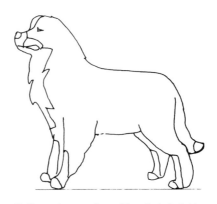

B. Correct proportion of length to height

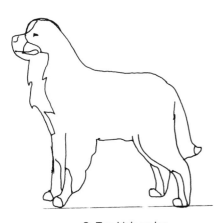

C. Too high on leg

Correct front

Correct front movement when dog
begins gaiting

Correct front movement at increased speed

This dog is too wide in front, lacks depth
of chest and appears out at elbow.

Toeing in

99

Toeing out

Valgus angulation is a specific deformity not to be confused with toeing out.

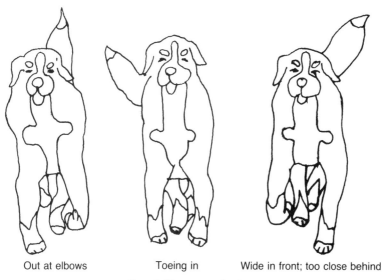

| Out at elbows | Toeing in | Wide in front; too close behind |

Fig. 17. **Movement Faults**

A Bernese exhibiting the faults shown in Fig. 17.

Fig. 18. This dog is "tied" at the elbows, which causes a "snatching" movement from side to side.

A Bernese exhibiting the faults shown in Fig. 18.

Fig. 19. A. Moving out at elbow. B. Moving wide in front. This front never converges enough during movement, rendering the dog constantly out of balance.

moderation. A true "toeing out" front will not be corrected by the chest dropping at maturity. Do not confuse "east-west" fronts with valgus angulation. Valgus angulation is a deformity that can occur in any large breed and Bernese are not immune. It is an external rotation of the radius bone in the leg. The cause is not clear; perhaps they inherit a tendency that can be stimulated by an injury or diet. This can occur in just one or both front legs.

Moving

Front movement faults can take many forms. The examples on pp. 101–03 are a few of the ones I have observed as common among Bernese Mountain Dogs and illustrates the fault in three movement drawings and then shows an actual dog with the fault.

The other front movement faults usually occur alone and not in combination as the aforestated, so one drawing will suffice.

I have also observed crossing over in the front. A dog that crosses overshoots the imaginary center line and instead of one foot being placed in front of another, one foot crosses the path of the other. This fault results in considerable waste of action.

Correct rear, standing   Correct rear, moving

Fig. 20. Correct rear, moving. The pads are clearly visible as each foot is lifted as legs angle toward the center line of gravity with no interference.

REARS

Standing

As in the case of fronts, the natural stance for a good rear is parallel with toes just slightly off vertical for balance.

The correct rear assembly also converges toward the center line with increased speed.

Proper rears when moving converge but do not "move close." A dog that is close in the rear often brushes its hocks on one another as it moves, or actually gets so close that it begins to interfere or cross over in the rear. This fault is quite common in Bernese and

"Barrel hocked" or "spread hocked" rear

Narrow rear

in fact occurs more often than not. I have seen judges so revolted by this that they have gone in the other direction and put up a spread-hocked dog. Many skillful handlers move dogs at a very rapid pace to try to hide close rears. They assume that if the judges never see the dog move slowly they will not be able to tell the difference between moving close and converging. I have also seen some clever judges get over this by asking the exhibitor to walk the dog, and thereby picking up the fault that others may have missed. Faulty rear stances are clues to faulty rear movement.

Moving

Common rear movement faults in Bernese Mountain Dogs (pp. 108–10).

106

"Toeing out"

SIDE GAIT

Once again good angulation and balance front and rear are essential ingredients in ample reach, drive and foot timing. Balance results in good foot timing. A dog that is overangulated in the rear may often compensate by kicking out in the rear and holding this

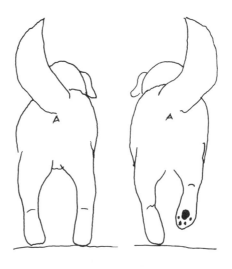

Fig. 21. "Barrel" or "spread" hocks are named for the distance between these joints standing or moving.

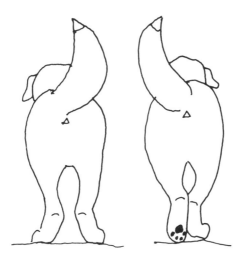

Fig. 22. "Cow hocks" are named for their similarity to the rear leg joints of a cow that needs milking.

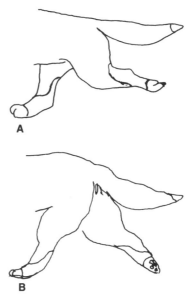

Fig. 23. In high-kicking rear movement the pads point upward (A) in wasted motion. A slow motion videotape would show this dog holding each hind foot up for a few seconds, waiting for the front foot to clear the path. While this is a very athletic compensation, it is wasted action no less. In correct rear movement (B), the pads should be clearly visible as the dog moves off.

The "flying trot" shows good reach in front and drive behind, and it is also executed with good foot timing.

high kick for a split second to allow the front foot to move out of the way so it will not interfere. This is often confused with rear drive. You can spot this high rear kick by looking for the pads when the dog moves away from you. They should be visible. If the dog is high kicking in the rear, they will not be visible.

Another type of wasted side gait action is lifting in the front or hackney gait. This is because of a lack of angulation in the shoulder. If you have ever observed a hackney pony or five-gaited horse in action you know that this is a very flashy step, and combined with the white feet of a Bernese, this improper movement has made a champion of many an undeserving dog. Judges are only human and many are drawn in by the flash. For the sake of a long-term breeding program I would avoid dogs with this fault as you may find yourself doubling up on this until you move yourself right out of the Winners circle. A well balanced Bernese can travel the mountains and fields all day without tiring. An unbalanced Bernese can be flashy and if moved quickly all that bobbing around can appear very athletic, but when slowed to a working trot the imbalance becomes evident. Look for that smooth, effortless, slow trot; it is the sign of a well-put-together dog. This is the dog to begin your breeding program with.

Reach and drive are also influenced by the length of upper arm and shoulder blade. For the best reach they should be equal in length. Many Bernese have a very long shoulder blade and a short upper arm causing a stilted gait. A few show the opposite condition. Select away from these toward equal length in shoulder blade and upper arm.

Ch. Cita v. Sagispicher (Wacho v. Tinosbach ex Deisi v. Sagispicher), owned by Kim Behrens and bred by Marianne Iff, is a Best in Show winner, handled by Bobbi Kinley. *Chuck Tatham*

4

Show Ring Competition

_____

INTRODUCTION

The sport of showing dogs has swallowed up more than one unsuspecting pet owner. Everyone starts out as a pet owner in one way or another. It starts when you take your pet to a local fun match and win a ribbon, then it's on to sanctioned matches and perhaps a puppy Group placement. Someone at the match suggests you should subscribe to the *Match Show Bulletin* and get a little handling under your belt since you have a promising puppy. Before you know it, you're on your way to the big time—point shows!

The prospect of your first show is intimidating: How do you get an entry form? After you finally get one, how do you fill it out? When you get there, how do you know when to go back in the ring? Soon you'll be entering shows like a pro and taking home the points. Now you're looking for a show within driving distance every weekend. After all, everyone says your dog looks good, better keep him out till he's finished. Summer is coming and he'll blow his coat. You enter every possible weekend until you finally come home with that elusive AKC champion title. Now what? He's a champion? Better get another puppy so you can finish him; after all you must have a good eye—look how quickly your first one finished. This breed needs you!

Guess what? You're hooked! This is the end of life as the rest of the world knows it. Unless your first champion was a homebred (very rare), you are now out to breed a champion of your own or perhaps a great dog to do some Group winning. Before you know it, you're on the phone with other breeders and exhibitors sharing health information and notes on puppy buyers. You have a dog in every room in your house, you're building kennels to make room for that great stud fee pup you just couldn't pass up and all of your family waits to make plans until the premium list is out so you won't miss a great judging lineup. If this sounds like heaven, by all means read on. If this sounds like hell, skip this chapter because there are few sports as addictive as the sport of dogs.

EARLY SHOW TRAINING

You've decided this is just your cup of tea? Well, let's start at the beginning, if I can remember back that far (oh, I forgot— it's the same with every new puppy). The most important part of showing a dog is attitude. A great outgoing, showy attitude can make a mediocre dog look good and a good dog look terrific. Bernese need that edge in the show ring as they can be ''standoffish.'' Start early when they are babies to get them to focus on you. The way to their attention span is through their stomachs.

Since we all have lives outside the dog world, I find the best way to train show dogs is to work it into your daily routine. If you have to set aside special times for training you'll never get around to it. I begin bait training, getting the dog's attention in the ring with food (yes, it's perfectly legal and everyone does it), in the kitchen at night when I prepare dinner. The pup or puppies are brought in the kitchen and I simply prepare dinner. Of course with all the food smells, they are quite keen, so I ask them if they want a treat and of course they stare at me blankly. Then I give them a few morsels and they start to put two and two together. Your puppy will begin to follow you everywhere in hopes of another treat. Now begins the training.

I begin by telling the puppy to stand. If he happens, by chance, to stand he will get a treat immediately; if not, I gently place my foot under his abdomen and ask him to stand while lifting him with my foot. As soon as the puppy is on his feet, he is rewarded with a treat. This continues for a few days or weeks depending on how quickly he catches on. I then begin to do the same thing while he is wearing a show collar with lead dangling. Then I begin picking up the end of the lead occasionally. If he tries to jump up, I gently nudge him down with my knee. No matter how unruly he is, I keep this a happy time with no stern corrections. This training is important; it will make you look like a competent handler. If you can communicate with your dog in the ring you'll have that little edge. I've had many people in the past compliment me on my handling skills and ask me to show their dogs—but this early training is what gave me the skills, not any aptitude as a handler.

Once the pup is used to receiving treats or bait while I'm holding the lead, I begin to direct him with the lead, pull him in a little closer, put my foot between his front feet to make him set his front, lift my leg and use my foot gently on the side of his rump to make him move to the left or right and just in general get him used to lead commands and subtle messages I want him to pick up on in the ring. All of this comes in small doses while I cook dinner every night. Hey, what could be easier—everybody's got to eat!

The next stage of training is either handling classes or match shows. Handling classes are usually run by all-breed clubs and may be taught by someone completely unfamiliar with Bernese Mountain Dogs. This is not important. You attend these classes so your dog will get used to the distraction of another dog running in front of him and behind him (so don't get in the front of the line). You're also there to have someone examine your dog so he will get used to strangers touching him, opening his mouth and checking for testicles if he's a male. If you happen to end up in a large class where the instructor only has time to go over your dog once or twice a night, ask someone in the class to go over your dog and tell them you will be happy to return the favor. This will give you both more of what you're there for. When the instructor does go over your dog, be sure to mention that Bernese are a full dentition breed so the entire bite should be checked, not just the front teeth.

Ch. De-Li's Foreign Touch (Bev's Black Jack v. BB ex Ch. Tonia v. Barenried) owned and bred by Lilian Ostermiller and handled here by Michelle Ostermiller, achieved success as a show dog, but more importantly, had thirty-seven offspring that became conformation champions and ten that made the grade in obedience.

John L. Ashbey

Ch. Shersan's Black Tie Required (Ch. Shersan's Change O'Pace v. Halidom, CD, ex Ch. Halidom Keri), owned and bred by Robert and Carolyn Kinley and handled by Bobbi Kinley. *John L. Ashbey*

117

Showing a Full Dentition Bite

You should practice showing the bite in this manner at home at an early stage. Take it slow and easy as Bernese can be quite stubborn about this. If you are consistent, your dog will eventually cooperate.

Another component to practice at home before attending class is gaiting. Whenever you gait your dog for a judge in the ring or for your handling instructor, the dog should always be between you and the judge.

Gaiting Patterns for the Ring

There are four basic gaiting patterns used most often in the ring: triangle, L, down and back, circle. A word of caution about the L pattern. If you are taught to change hands in your handling

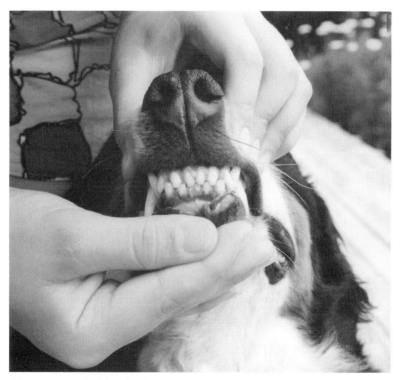

The correct method for showing the bite to the judge is to lift the lips in front of the muzzle and pull down the lower lip to expose the incisors.

To show full dentition, lift the side curtains of the mouth and pull down the bottom lip.

class, and are lucky enough to find yourself in the Group ring, don't do it. These are big dogs and switching hands will break their gait. If you find yourself between the dog and the judge, simply move ahead or behind your dog. Professional handlers in the Working Group rarely switch hands on the L, and you want to look as good as the pros.

When you practice these patterns you should always know where the judge or instructor is standing, since you want them to be able to see the dog, not you. Take care to run in a straight line, for if you are weaving around as you run, you will adversely affect your dog's gait. I use a little helper to remain straight. I look for something directly ahead of me and keep my eye on it while running

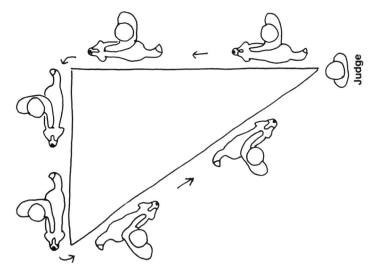

The triangle pattern is commonly used in the show ring and allows the gait to be observed from the front, rear and side without risking the dog breaking stride.

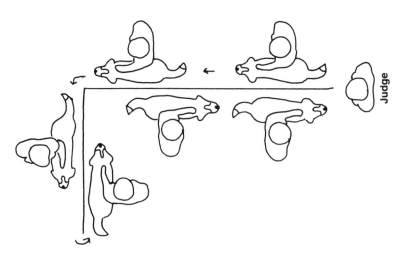

The "L" pattern is useful for observing movement from both sides and is used most often in the Group ring.

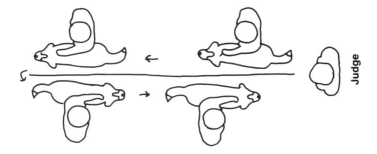

The "Down and Back" is simply moving in a straight line away from the judge and back again. This pattern allows the judge to concentrate on front and rear movement and is often referred to as "coming and going" for obvious reasons.

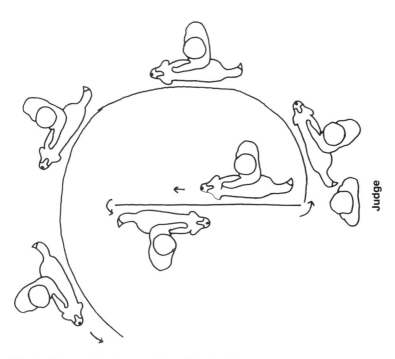

The circle is used to observe side gait in the individual dog, often following the "Down and Back," or to compare a group of dogs all moving together. In the show ring the direction of the circle is *always* counterclockwise.

straight toward it. This keeps me from looking down at the dog and weaving to compensate for what I anticipate my dog is going to do. This also prevents the bad habit of staring at the judge or instructor while moving. Some people manage to run and never take their eyes off the judge, smiling the entire time as if to say "Look at me." I find this distracts from the dog and many judges find it offensive. To check on your straight line movement, run toward a mirror. You will pick up any of your dog's front movement faults at the same time. Knowing your dog's faults is a very important part of successful showing. If you can asses your dog's strong points and the competition's weak points, you can amplify your dog's assets. For example, you're standing ringside before your class is called. You look around at all your competitors and notice they have dippy toplines, while your dog has a level back. When you get in the ring, a couple of quick runs of your hand down the dog's back near decision time will often draw the judge's eye to your dog's topline and may put you in the Winners circle. In point shows the judge only has about two minutes to judge a dog, so a little help doesn't hurt. Just keep it subtle; no judge wants the feeling of being told what to do!

Your mirror also comes in handy for stacking. Your puppy is already used to standing from your kitchen training; now comes the serious business of setting his feet. Have your puppy stand next to you on your left and put your mirror far enough away on your left to see your puppy's entire body in the reflection. Take the collar, not the lead, in your right hand; lean over and lift the pup's left front leg at the elbow and position it in a straight line with the tip of the shoulder blade. When viewed from the front, his feet should point straight ahead and his legs should point straight ahead and his legs should be set a comfortable distance apart. Be careful not to set the front too wide or too narrow. The rear is set by leaning over the dog and taking hold of the hock and positioning it perpendicularly to the ground. Be careful to set the rear at a comfortable distance from the front. If you pull the rear out too far, the dog will lean back in the front, resembling a rocking or "hobby horse." You can monitor all this by checking your mirror. Your dog may have to maintain this position in the ring for fairly long periods of time, so get him used to doing so. If he moves a foot, you quietly say "Nooo," and reposition that foot while feeding him treats and

Setting the front

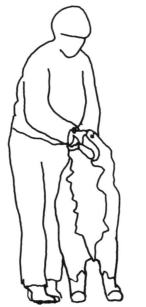

The front set at the correct width

Setting the rear

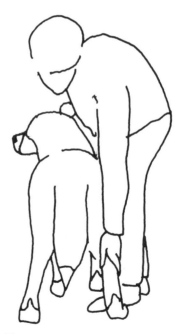

The rear set at the correct width

praising him. If he's a natural at this, you may try going out to the end of a short show lead and baiting him with treats, all the while asking him to maintain this position. Training your Bernese to do this will enable you to keep him in a show pose and watching you while all the other dogs in the ring are relaxed and looking sloppy. Remember, once again, "two minutes a dog"—a little help never hurts!

Now that you and your dog have honed your skills, it is time for a trial run. Match shows are the place. Most handling classes can fill you in about publications in your area that list matches coming up, or you can contact one of the regional Bernese clubs closest to you for possible Bernese matches, often called "Bernerfests." (See Bibliography for club listings.) Match shows are practice shows; you can enter them on the same day as you show, but there are no set ring times, so plan to spend the day. There is usually a cutoff time of about twelve noon when the sponsoring club stops taking entries. Generally, about an hour later judging begins.

Entries are simple. You need only list your dog's name and the class you wish to enter: Puppy 3 to 6 (months of age), Puppy 6 to 9 and Puppy 9 to 12. If you have an adult or puppy over one year, the class name is Adult. Entries are also divided by sex. Males compete with males, females with females, and the winner in each sex competes for Best of Breed. Entry fees are nominal, usually about five to six dollars for each dog.

If your dog is chosen Best of Breed, you will then have to wait for the rest of the Working dogs to be judged and compete in the Working Group against all the other breed winners in the same age division. The winner of the Working Group will then compete for Best in Match. There are usually two Best in Match winners, Best Puppy and Best Adult.

Matches are fun outings and a great time to spend one-on-one with your Berner. Do your best to make them fun. Your dog will probably enjoy showing at matches, and this will reflect favorably on how he behaves later in point shows. Match show judges can be AKC-approved judges gaining experience for breeds for which they plan to apply, or they can be breeders with solid knowledge in one breed perhaps totally unrelated to Bernese. Matches are practice grounds (for dogs, handlers and judges) and what happens there may or may not be an accurate reflection of the quality of any one dog. There are few breeds that mature as slowly or go through the "uglies" like a Bernese Mountain Dog. Keep this in mind and don't be dissuaded by comments from people in other breeds. Some of the Best in Show dogs in this book, including my own, went through terrible growth stages. As an example, consider the following photos of the top winning Bernese Mountain Dog to date, available through the generosity of his owner, Carolyn Kinley.

The early photos gave no hint of what was to come. Pace earned twenty Bests in Show in his career and was the only Bernese to date to win the Working Group at Westminster. So keep the faith, Rome wasn't built in a day. Limit your showing to matches now and then until your dog is mature; unless he is an outstanding puppy, you should wait to enter point shows. A mature dog filled out and in his prime can often finish his championship in four to six shows. An immature dog can take as many as thirty shows or more. Entries cost the same win or lose, so why waste the money and time. I know it's hard to be patient, but it's well worth the wait to hear, "Wow, where did that beautiful dog come from?"

GROOMING

Teeth

A breed with a full dentition bite particularly benefits from clean teeth when competition is keen. You will find it much easier to keep oral hygiene up weekly or monthly. If it gets out of hand you will have to have your dog's teeth cleaned by your vet and this often requires anesthesia. Cleaning teeth is easy and requires either some old scaling tools from your dentist or from one of the kennel supply catalogs. Simply scrape the tartar off, just as your dentist does on your own teeth. Start at the top of the tooth just under the gum line using a hooked dental tool behind the tartar and pulling down the face of the tooth. Continue all around the tooth until it is clean. Repeat the same process around all sides of the tooth. Try not to trigger any bleeding. After cleaning wipe gums with a little Listerine on a cotton ball.

At 14 months

At two years

The celebrated Best in Show Berner, Ch. Shersan's Change O' Pace v. Halidom, CD, went through the same growth stages others of his breed go through. The photos above and on page 128 show "Pacer" going from developing youngster to his full estate of adult beauty. They underline the wisdom of restraint and showing a dog only when he is really ready.

At two and a half years—a new champion

At almost five years—a multiple BIS dog

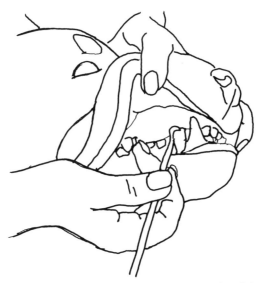

Regular use of a dental scaler is basic to good oral hygiene for all dogs. A puppy can, and should, be taught to stand quietly while his teeth are being worked on. Clean teeth are an asset to a show dog and a safeguard for overall good health.

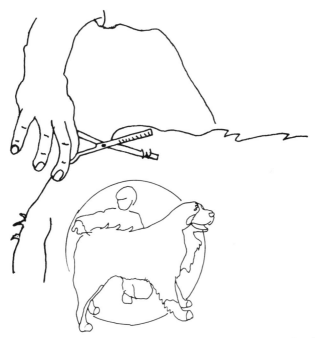

Some Bernese coats will grow especially thick over the hindquarters. Careful use of a pair of thinning shears will greatly enhance the overall outline of such a dog.

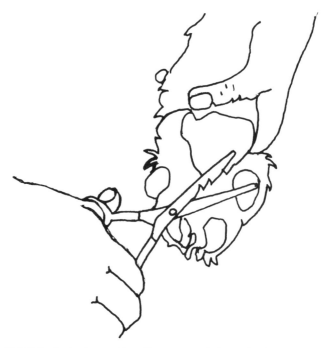

With straight barber's shears, trim off any excess hair growing between the pads of the feet. This will make the dog more comfortable, improve the appearance of the feet and may even provide better traction on slippery floor mats.

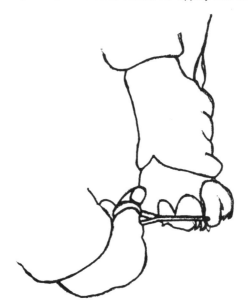

Trim back the hair around the feet to provide a rounded, compact look.

Trimming?

"Bernese should be shown in a natural state without undue trimming . . ." That is what the Standard calls for and I agree—to a point. But when this works against the dog's true structure, I go back to my judging experience and the two minute rule and then come up with the phrase "A little help never hurts!" Let's face it, if you went to a stock car race with a true "stock" car and engine, what are your odds of winning? This no-trimming policy might work if no one trimmed—but most do!

Do try to keep trimming to a minimum, but do what is necessary to show your Berner to his or her best advantage! If your dog has a level back but is plagued by a thick coat over the rump that stands up and makes him appear high behind, by all means thin the hair so you can show off that beautiful topline. The judge may forget to feel to see if your dog is high in the rear. Or, in a large class, he may check and, then, at the last minute when he pulls you up next to another dog with a level topline, forget it was only hair and place you second. Judges are only human; they get sick, have bad days and memory lapses like anyone else. Don't expect them to see and find everything about every dog.

On the feet the hair is removed between the pads and the foot is rounded to accentuate the natural arch. Thinning the hair around the neck will help clean up a stuffy-looking neck. Backs of the hocks should be brushed up, then trimmed perpendicularly with the ground. All trimming should be done with the grain of the hair. Look for the direction in which the hair lays and cut from underneath in the opposite direction parallel to the hair. The best thinning shears to use are called 44-20s. They cut very little hair so you will not be able to make any very serious mistakes. Practice your trimming at home well in advance of a dog show, so if you happen to remove too much hair, it will have time to grow back in before showing.

Whiskers or Not?

As an exhibitor, I was always very careful to remove all whiskers before any of my dogs ever entered the show ring. It was a necessary part of grooming a dog for the ring. Since I began judging, I find I can never remember if a dog had its whiskers removed or

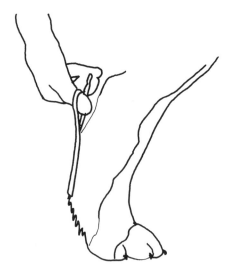

Trim the backs of the hocks on a straight line, but avoid a "barbered" look.

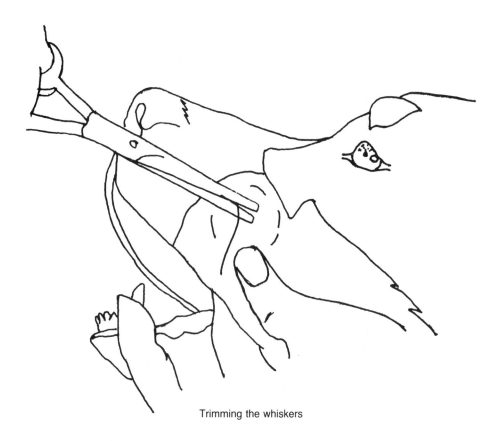

Trimming the whiskers

not—it just doesn't matter. Therefore, I very seldom remove whiskers anymore. Why bother if the judge doesn't notice. Also, whiskers are sensory organs, the dog does use them, so why deprive him of them. However, if your dog has a lovely clean, white blaze with two to three distracting black or brown corkscrew whiskers, these should be removed. Also trim if your dog looks more like an otter than a Bernese with a gaggle of long, entwined whiskers. This is easy to do, but is best done in small doses as dogs get bored and fidgety with this procedure. A grooming table is the best place for this trimming. Hook your dog to the arm by his collar and use a strong light so you can see easily. Place your fingers behind his lip, roll the whisker out and cut as close to the skin as possible without cutting any of the short hairs on his muzzle.

Coat Care

The two secrets of coat care are cleanliness and moisture. Clean coats don't break. Thus, if you keep the coat clean you will achieve the maximum length. The way to keep the coat clean is by regular bathing using a moisturizing shampoo. Should the coat feel dry, a glycerine rinse (about one quarter cup to a gallon) will make it supple without weighing it down and making it greasy. A bath about every two weeks, or every week if you are showing, is often enough. To keep the coat healthy in between shampoos, keep a misting bottle filled with water handy, and whenever you happen to think about it, mist your Berner as you would your houseplants. The coat will be moisture-rich and this will also keep it from breaking. If you find occasional dandruff try a "people" cure. I find that Head and Shoulders Scalp Moisturizing Shampoo in the blue bottle works wonders on Berners!

When grooming the Bernese coat, brush the hair from the tail toward the neck. This sounds odd but try it; you'll see that it has a natural tendency to go that way. I have my suspicions as to how this practice began, but it is here to stay and actually works quite well, particularly if your dog has a dip behind the withers you need to cover. After bathing your Berner you can either let him air-dry if it is warm enough or blow him dry with a commercial dryer. Whichever method you choose, you can take a small slicker brush and back-brush the legs while the dog is drying. This will cause

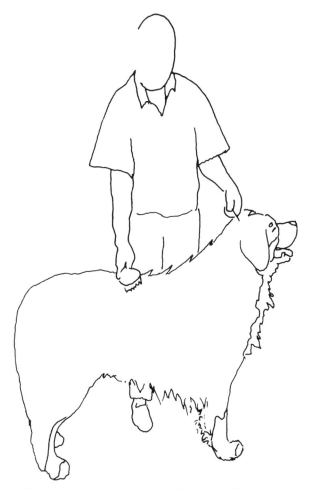

Brush the coat against the natural lie, from tail to head.

the hair on the legs to dry puffed out and give the maximum volume to the look of bone in the legs. Start at the tip of the toe and brush all around the entire leg up to the elbow or just below. The rest of the coat is brushed forward all around the body. If you are blowing your dog dry, blow right behind the brush. I strongly recommend blowing Bernese dry, as it gives you the opportunity to inspect their skin and check for any skin conditions or external parasites that are otherwise impossible to see through the dense black coat. The blower is so strong that it actually parts the hair down to the skin as you go.

On the day of the show, repeat this grooming procedure, add-

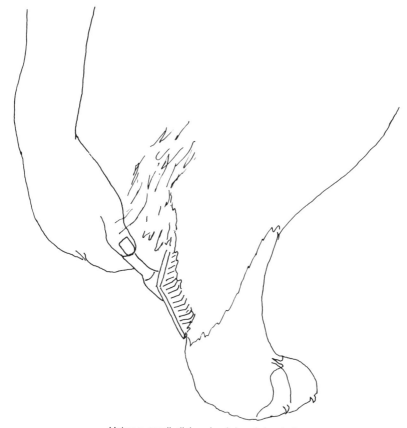
Using a small slicker, back brush leg hair.

ing a little texturizer to your water spray bottle to help give the coat more volume. Test the texturizer at home to make sure it isn't too heavy. If it weighs the coat down, try thinning it with more water until you come up with just the right concentration, or switch to another brand. You may also want to bring your blower along to help raise spots that have been flattened by being pressed against the side of the crate.

Nutrition is a very important part of good coat condition. You always get what you put in. A poor diet shows up in the coat first. I recommend a natural dry food with no preservatives, no soy, no corn and no wheat. If this sounds impossible, read the labels. There are foods manufactured that are not based on corn and wheat. I use a conditioning food with a brown rice base. I also give a daily supplement of 30 to 50 mgs. of zinc for coat and skin, as well as 500 units Vitamin C (for flexibility) and 400 units Vitamin E (as an anti-oxidant). Should you find the zinc and Vitamin C lying at the bottom of the bowl, crush them first and sprinkle them over the top, or simply slip your index finger behind your dog's top canine tooth, raise the top jaw and drop the pills in the back of the throat.

It has also been my experience that Bernese, particularly males, have a sixth sense when it comes to staying in condition for the show ring. Somehow they sense that now is the time to become a picky eater because you will try anything to get them to eat and stay in top condition. You begin to realize just how intelligent this breed is, as your Berner watches you mixing in a new type of food at every meal to try to entice him to eat. You'll stumble on some new canned food that makes him wolf his ration down, only to watch him turn up his nose after you've stocked up on thirty cans. This game is a favorite of many top winning Berners so don't feel you have been singled out. Try to wait him out, but you may have to play along for as long as you are showing. Variety seems to be the key, and chicken is a favorite mixer. Should you have the opposite problem—too much weight (this occurs more often in females)—try cutting down on the dry food and mixing it with a can of green beans. Your girl is not starving and there are very few calories in green beans. Rawhide bones play havoc with leg hair so avoid them while maintaining a show coat. If your dog is bored with long hours traveling to shows or lying in his crate, try broccoli stems or carrots as toys. Many Berners love them, they won't stick in the coat and, in a breed prone to cancer, they are wonderful cancer fighters. Chew hooves are also good substitutes, and contain no nutrition. However, even those chubby show girls can enjoy broccoli and carrots with no fear of adding too many calories.

The bane of many a seasoned exhibitor in many breeds, not just Bernese, is hot spots. Hot spots can occur when you least expect them. Some conditions that can trigger these troublesome spots of moist eczema are long wet periods (standing out in the rain all day) followed by air drying in a warm room. If your Berner is somehow left out in the wet weather for an extended period, towel dry him thoroughly or blow him dry, and leave him in a well-ventilated area until he is thoroughly dry. Another cause is not combing out all the dead undercoat when your Berner begins to shed. This hair matted close to the skin can cause moisture and bacteria to collect under it, prime conditions for a hot spot. Keep dead hair raked out or combed out and check spots that mat easily, such as under the ear flaps and under the elbows. Sometimes hot spots seem to just appear for no known reason. Some hot spots respond well to a topical spray of Gentocin; others require shaving and treatment by a veterinarian. This will also shave a hole in your dog's show career and put him on the sidelines until his coat grows back. Do your best to head off hot spots before they have a chance to get started. If your dog is prone to hot spots, try mixing some stewed tomatoes or tomato sauce in his food; this sometimes helps.

Ears

Whenever you shampoo your Berner, take great care not to get water in the ear canal. Moisture in the ear canal can lead to fungus and other infections. If the ears are dirty, use a damp washcloth with water and rub off the dirt gently. If the inside of the ears are dirty swab them out with a little peroxide on a soft cotton swab (do not go deep). When the ear is clean on the outside, it is important to keep it dry. There are many good commercial ear drying solutions and powders and even solutions that turn into powders deep in the ear canal. This will help prevent ear infections since bacteria and yeast multiply rapidly in moist ears. In a breed such as Bernese with an ear flap that keeps the ear dark and moist with limited airflow, weekly or biweekly use of ear powder is a good preventive measure. Trimming some of the hair away from the canal opening can also help, particularly if the hair is profuse. Avoid the use of creams, as they often aggravate the problem.

One of the characteristics of Bernese Mountain Dogs, rarely discussed as of late, are ear fuzzles. Ear fuzzles are tufts of hair that grow on the tops of the ear flaps. This was once a coveted feature of the breed but is now routinely removed to give a neater appearance in the show ring. This is rather sad, but true, as it could have become an outstanding breed characteristic much like the highly prized ear fringing on Papillons. Today, Berners that are shown with their ear fuzzles intact often look strangely out of place. To neaten up the ear, thin the fuzzles with your thinning shears, then gently pull the remaining stray hairs by hand. Neaten around

Use thinning shears on the backs of a dog's ears and where they join the skull to enhance placement and overall well-groomed appearance.

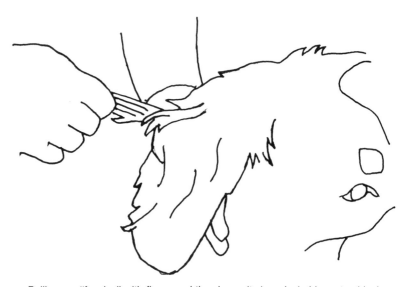

Pulling ear "fuzzles" with finger and thumb results in a desirable, natural look.

138

the edges of the ear with your thinning shears, but not too neat; this should look natural. Lift the ear flap and thin out the thick hair under the ear so the ear will lay correctly. When you retire your dog from the show ring, grow the longest possible ear fuzzles you can get!

Nail Care

Long toenails can cause a well-arched foot to become splayed (toes spread out and foot flattened), so it is important to keep a Berner's nails short. This breed can often have very heavy bone causing a tendency toward a splayed foot. The correct foot is tight and has a nice arch. Start early with weekly or biweekly nail clipping or grinding. Human nail clippers work well on very young puppies. When this is no longer effective, it's time to progress to a nail clipper or grinder. If you have a grooming table, this is a good time to acquaint your pup with its use. I find the grinder to be the most satisfactory method for shortening nails. It automatically cauterizes the vein in the nail should you cut too close. The grinder also gives a smooth, rounded appearance to the nail with no jagged edges often left with clippers. The only drawback is the noise, so start early to familiarize your Berner with the grinder's sound and vibration. Introduce it slowly. If your Berner is just too stressed by this, you may have to stick with clippers. Either method works and the important part is just getting the job done!

There is a vein in each nail and if cut too closely, it will bleed. Whenever you cut nails keep a coagulant handy and apply as needed, using direct pressure to the nail.

POINT SHOW PROCEDURE

You've practiced at handling classes, taught yourself all the grooming tricks through trial and error and attended lots of matches. Your Berner has been high in the rear, lost his neck, had no legs, then nothing but legs, and now seems to have leveled out in all areas as well as filled out in body. You are both ready for point shows, but how do you get an entry blank? The surest method is to subscribe to *Pure-Bred Dogs—American Kennel Gazette*. This publication includes a separate Events Calendar that lists upcoming shows, judges panels and locations. In the *Gazette* you will find the names and addresses of annually licensed superintendents. These are the people who send out premium lists and entry forms and who receive your entries (unless the club giving the show is self-superintended). If you are in a hurry call someone you've met at a match who regularly attends point shows and ask them for the phone number of the superintendent who handles most of the shows in your area. Call the superintendent and ask to be placed on the mailing list for upcoming shows.

After you receive the premium list, you will need some knowledge of dog shows to fill out the entry form.

Each class has a purpose, with some more useful and popular than others. Puppy is for dogs under a year old. Just like at match shows, the class is divided by age, but a puppy must be at least six months of age to be shown in a point show. Age is determined by the date of the show. You may enter a puppy who will be just six months on the day of the show, even though he is not six months at the time of entry. Entries have a time limit and must be mailed to arrive by a deadline known as the "closing date." This closing date occurs about three weeks prior to the date of the actual show and is published on the premium list and in the Events Calendar. The 12 to 18 Month class is a relatively new class for immature dogs too old for the puppy class. I have already stated my feelings about showing immature dogs. Unless a puppy is an incredibly early maturer, competing in puppy classes should be reserved for the national or regional Specialty shows sponsored by the Bernese Mountain Dog Club of America. These shows are gatherings of Berner folk who know how these dogs mature, and among puppies of a similar age your ugly duckling may be the standout. This is a truly unusual breed for swans from ugly ducklings, so be patient. Many Bernese Specialties are won by a dog from the Veterans class—maturity is late coming. The Novice class is for inexperienced dogs that have no points—does this sound perfect? Not so fast! The Novice class often suggests just that, novice all around. Why use this one when you've gotten so much practice by now. Of course if you skipped over all that practice stuff and have decided to just go right ahead and enter a point show, use this class so you won't be humiliated. Dog people take shows very seriously and foolish mistakes in the ring are not lightly excused. The Bred by Exhibitor class is for the breeder of the dog to handle in—the breeder is also the exhibitor. But it is more involved than it appears, as the dog must also be owned by the breeder, co-owned by the breeder or owned by a member of the breeder's immediate family. The American-bred class is for dogs born in the United States as a result of a mating that occured in the United States. The Open class is open to all dogs, including champions. I enter this class under judges who may be judging in my area for the first time, since it usually has the largest entry of mature dogs, and the winner of this class is most often awarded the points in Winners class. For Winners, all of the winners of the same set in the previous classes are returned to the ring for Winners competition. There are two Winners classes, one for dogs and one for bitches (females). The Winners Dog is awarded the points based on the number of males in competition; the Reserve Winners Dog is next in line should the Winners Dog be disqualified. The same applies to Winners Bitch, only her points are based on the number of females in competition. Best of Winners can be awarded to either Winners Dog or Winners Bitch. The Best of Winners award grants the greatest number of points (if there is a difference) to the dog so named. Example: You are showing a male. There is only one other male entered and your dog is Winners Dog for 1 point. When you return to the ring for Best of Breed competition, your dog goes Best of Winners. If there were enough females present to give the Winners Bitch five points, your male would now have 5 points to his credit instead of his original 1 point. The point schedule varies from one part of the country to another but is always published in the catalog. Should you have no one with you to mark the catalog (on sale at all point shows) and you are unsure of the number of dogs in the ring, you may go to the superintendent's office and look up the markings (the pages from the judge's book). Check these pages for absentees, as your points are based on the number of dogs that were actually shown, not the number entered. If you have been lucky enough to win Best of Breed you may also count the "Specials" or finished champions entered in competition in your points, but they still remain divided by sex.

If your Berner wins the "Breed" (as it is often referred to by seasoned exhibitors), he is now eligible to compete in the Working Group. There are presently eighteen breeds in the Working Group and the best examples of all or most will be your competition. Should your dog be fortunate enough to take a Group first, you must stay for Best in Show. There are seven dogs in Best in Show competition, one from each Group including your dog representing the Working Group. Best in Show is the highest honor a dog may receive at any one show, and if your Berner takes a "Best" he will enter a very select circle that, as of this writing, consists of only thirteen dogs since 1977. Congratulations!

5

Obedience and the
Bernese Mountain Dog

INTRODUCTION

Bernese Mountain Dogs are a sensitive breed, sometimes dis-
guised by a well-developed stubborn streak. Despite prior experiences you may have had with the choke-collar jerk method of
obedience training, you may be surprised at how ineffective it can
be on Bernese Mountain Dogs. I learned this the hard way. I had
trained many Golden Retrievers in this manner and was so effective
at it that I trained dogs for other people and taught classes, as well
as putting titles on my own dogs.

Naturally, when I brought my first Bernese Mountain Dog
home at five months of age and fifty-five pounds, I decided this
was going to be a lot of dog so I had better enroll him in an obedience
class and get him under control early. Much to my surprise my
handling skills seemed to have no effect. He refused to sit, and if
he did happen to plop down out of exhaustion, he did so in the
crookedest manner possible. Whenever I turned my head for a second he would lunge on top of another dog. He made me look like

Liskarn American Bound Jerry, Am., Can. CD, DD, owned by Sara Dombroski, Alison Jaskiewicz (his trainer) and Deborah Mulvey, proudly displays the rosette he won when he became the first Bernese to earn a perfect 200 score.

a rank amateur who had never handled a dog before. One night after four or five classes (with no improvement) the instructor yelled at me to make my dog sit straight! I couldn't take it any more and replied in frustration, "I can't make him sit at all let alone straight!" At this point it was suggested that I resort to a prong collar. I had used a prong collar before with terrific results, so I agreed and the next day I was off to buy one. That very evening I headed for the practice field, Berner in tow, with my new prong collar. I fitted my unruly Berner with his new collar, positioned him on my left side and stepped off briskly on my left foot while singing out "Heel" in my best "up," happy training voice, and giving a good "come along" jerk. I was stopped dead in my tracks! Turning, I saw my unruly Berner on his back, all four feet in the air as if he were dead! I ran back to him and took off the collar, and he immediately leapt to his feet, chattered his teeth at me and began running around. Figuring I had jerked too hard I started the same process all over again, with all of the same results, so I gave up! I decided that Bernese were wonderful house dogs, great companions and that they could not be obedience trained.

After much discussion with people who had the same experience, I came to the conclusion that it was not the breed that had the problem, but the method. Pain does not work, reward does. Now, all my dogs are trained by the method of "only encouragement." I ignore their mistakes, encourage them to do it right and reward them with food when they do. They are happy workers and well-disciplined animals that are welcomed wherever they go.

BASIC TRAINING

A puppy at eight weeks of age has her full complement of brain power and, like a human youngster, is a sponge ready to soak up all you have to offer. She is a pack animal and you are the pack leader. She will gladly focus all her attention on you now as at no other period in her life. Don't waste this precious time, start basic obedience now, before she has a chance to become big and hard to handle. Start your first training sessions with your new puppy just as you do in show training, by working it into your daily schedule. Begin by putting a buckle collar on your puppy and letting her wear it around in your presence. When you find you'll be working on a project in one room for an extended period of time, begin lead breaking your pup. I find this is easily accomplished by attaching a lead to her collar, giving just enough length to allow her to lie down comfortably and attaching the other end of the lead to a door knob. The reasoning behind this is to make your pup's first restrainer an unknown. She can struggle and test the door knob, not you! She will struggle, go to the end of the lead and vigorously try to free herself. When she finally gives in and lies down quietly, you can go to her, praise her and end the lesson. After a few lessons like this, walking with you will be a lot more fun and restraint will be calmly accepted. Continue to keep your Berner on a buckle collar until she is quite familiar with walking on a lead, and encourage her to stay on your left using treats and generous praise. The hallways of your home make great places to train a puppy to come when you call. Put the pup at the end of a hallway, go to the other end and call her (with a treat in your pocket, of course). When she finally gets to you, lavish with praise and reward with a treat. You'll find her speed improving a little at a time. Be patient—once she learns it she'll never forget. While you're in the hallway try throwing a small wooden dumbbell, glove or anything else you may have around that will resemble later obedience equipment. If she picks it up, make a big fuss; if she runs off with it, don't worry. Follow her, take it from her and start over. Make it a game. At this point just holding something in her mouth is a big success. More often than not Bernese are not natural retrievers, but this early play training can help. This early training should be one-on-one with no other dogs or family members to distract the pup or you. Work on the basics—sit, stand and come. A puppy with only this basic training from eight weeks to four months of age will become a reasonable canine good citizen, as long as you work with your pup from ten to fifteen minutes daily during this period.

All new pups will do things that are inappropriate to your lifestyle and there must be a word to signal your disapproval. The best word is one you will never use in simple conversation— "Nooo!" As soon as you use the "Big Nooo," you should immediately substitute acceptable behavior and change immediately to a high-pitched, happy voice when she takes the cue. For example, the pup takes a family member's shoe to her area and begins to chew. You quickly pick up one of her toys or a chew bone and say "Nooo!" Now remove the shoe, substitute the proper item and say "Good dog." Train yourself to do this quickly and cleanly; do not dwell on the "Nooo!" Do dwell on the happy "Good dog." In this way you can also substitute any positive behavior for any undesirable behavior you wish to correct. Next time, if your pup ignores the shoe and picks up something of her own, this should also be praised. Praise does not have to be used only in conjunction with a correction.

At four months of age you may find your model little pup turning into a monster. She is cutting teeth, won't come when called, is into everything and has gotten very stubborn. Your training will become a little firmer now. You can now give her an upward tug

146

on the buckle collar to reinforce the correction, but be positive, as she can become very stubborn and negative at this point. This is the flight stage; hopefully your pup is responding well to the Come command by now.

If you and your puppy make it through the flight stage you should be prepared for the adolescent period. Your loving pup may know you one day and not the next. Her training will seem as though it was for nothing and she will jump sideways at the sight of a fire hydrant, telephone pole or you. You may never understand what is setting your dog off. This can occur at different times up until one and a half years of age. Be sure to keep her on a leash in strange surroundings, no matter how well trained she has been up until now. This stage will pass; just be patient and supportive. You will find this stage much easier to handle if you have faithfully performed your early obedience training. This is the worst possible time to enter a dog show in either obedience or conformation. Wait until this rebellious period passes before introducing your dog to such new, unknown experiences and unfamiliar surroundings.

EQUIPMENT

Your equipment should be lightweight for puppy training, advancing to heavier as your dog grows. Nylon is quite satisfactory. On very young puppies I often use a show lead that is extremely lightweight. The less connection they make between the lead and you, the better. They should focus on what you are saying more than on how you are physically conveying your commands.

BASIC HEELING

Simple heeling is taught with your dog on your left side. The leash is held in your right hand with the left hand resting on the lead above your dog's head. The left hand will let out or take up lead as needed. Ideally, in Heel position your dog's head is close to your left knee. When starting this exercise, stand your dog on your left; start out on your left foot to signal your intentions while singing out in a high, happy voice her name and the command

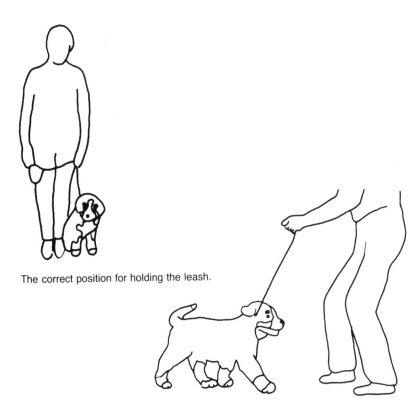

The correct position for holding the leash.

Running backward makes the training session an exciting game for the puppy.

Tap down the rear while pulling up gently on the collar.

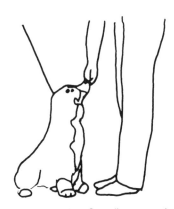

Finishing the "Come" command

148

"Heel." If she forges ahead, pat your knee and call her back into position. As soon as she is keeping up at your side, give a treat and praise but continue walking all the while. Should she lag behind repeat the same procedure of patting your knee, treat and praise. Keep your pace lively as Bernese can be very slow workers if allowed to get in the habit of responding lackadaisically. When working with a very young pup, keep her moving but don't set your pace so fast that she must run to keep up on the normal heel. Remember not to pull on the lead or keep the lead so tight that your pup is being dragged. Keep the lead loose, ask the pup to use her thinking cap to keep up. Surprise your pup with unexpected turns, to the right, to the left and totally turning around to go the other way. Always step into these turns with your left foot; if the pup is watching she will notice these and follow right along. If she does, a treat and a big fuss are in order. If she doesn't notice, call her along and when she is in step a treat and praise are called for once again. Ignore mistakes, reward successes! When making the left turn you will walk right into a pup that is not paying attention. Be careful not to step on her; take this turn carefully and deliberately.

THE COME OR RECALL

You can walk right into this from the basic Heel. As you are walking forward, your pup on the left moving at normal speed, you slow down to signal your intention to change and guide your pup around to your front. Now, starting on your left foot, begin running backward, at the same time using the high, singing voice to say her name and "Come." Let out plenty of lead and then begin to pull in lead, thereby gently reeling in your pup while you slow your backward pace. As soon as she is standing in front of you slip her a treat and generous praise. This is a more formal version of what she already learned in the hallway, so your pup should be very comfortable with this and proud of herself. Running away stimulates the pup and makes it a great game of catch that is hard to resist.

Keep it fun! If you go out to practice one day and the pup is not "with it," and you find yourself getting frustrated, stop at the end of an exercise and skip it for that day. One bad experience can scar a Bernese very badly and can take weeks or months of undoing.

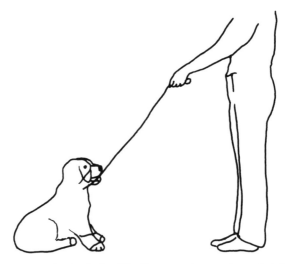

After your puppy understands the "Stay" command, go to the end of the leash.

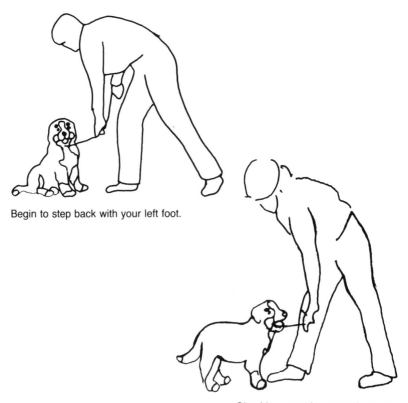

Begin to step back with your left foot.

Give him a *gentle* tug on the collar.

No matter how sure your pup may seem to be, remember she really is very sensitive.

THE SIT AND STAY

As soon as you have mastered the Come, you can begin to add the Sit. I like this series of exercises as one works right into another. You may run right along with these and let your pup set the pace. I find that all dogs like repetition, particularly when learning. It gives them the opportunity to do it right. Do the same things in the same order every day, so your puppy can anticipate, do it correctly and get a well-deserved treat. This pattern is also a good one because the exercises are not performed in this order in the obedience ring where it is important that the dog not anticipate and forge ahead to the next exercise without being given the command.

When you have begun the Come command and are running backward, start to pull up ever so gently on the lead so that when you come to a stop the pup receives a minor tug on the collar. At this moment you sing out her name and command ''Sit'' in your best high, happy voice, press lightly on her rump tapping her into the Sit position and following up immediately with a treat and praise. If she gets up, simply put her back in the Sit if only for a second. Say ''Good dog,'' and give a treat immediately. Have her hold the next Sit a second longer and stop training. Work gradually up to a few seconds sitting in front of you. Then, while she is sitting in front of you, say ''Stay.'' If she stays for a few seconds give a treat and lavish praise. Gradually work up to staying in a Sit for twenty to thirty seconds, then add a little twist. Walk away and stand at the end of the lead. At first she will want to follow. Put her back in the Sit-Stay and leave again. If she stays, give a treat and praise when you return. Don't call her to you. The Stay command means ''Stay were I put you until I return to you.'' Never invite your dog to break the Stay command.

After your pup has mastered the Stay command for a minute or thirty seconds, you may introduce a new word that means basically the same thing—''Wait.'' I prefer this command when I am going to follow up with another command. Example: You want to do a continuous routine and not finish up your training with a Sit-

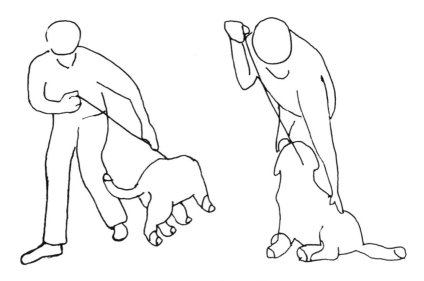

Step back to the standing position, turn the puppy
around and tuck him gently into a sit.

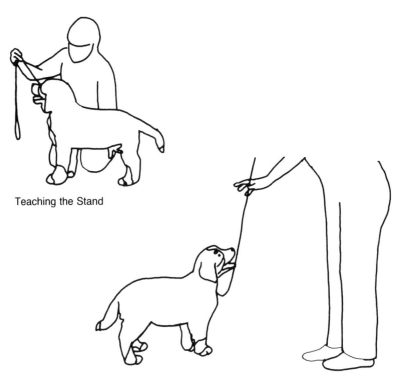

Teaching the Stand

Slowly work your way to the end of the lead.

Stay, but you would like your dog to do a series of Come commands. Simply call your pup to you, have her sit in front of you and say "Wait." Take a few steps backward, sing out her name and "Come" and reel her in or take up your lead slack again. When she sits in front of you give a treat. This will now lead you into the next exercise.

THE FINISH OR RETURN TO HEEL POSITION

Your pup is sitting in front of you and you would like her alongside so you can return to your heeling exercises. She already follows you whenever you take steps backward starting with your left foot, so take only one step back with your left foot and she will probably get up to follow. If not give a gentle tug on her buckle collar. Take the lead behind you with your left hand gently guiding her back with it. When she is even with your left foot, begin to guide forward. Pat your leg and coax her along in the beginning until she understands what you want. She will be turning around toward your left leg, which is still in the stepped-back position. As soon as she is facing forward, begin to step back into the standing position with your left foot, asking her to follow by patting your leg and calling to her. When your legs are back together and the pup is next to you on your left, gently tuck her into a Sit and give a treat and lots of praise.

You are now ready to sing out her name and the Heel command and step right off into your Heel exercises once again.

THE STAND AND STAY

I do not believe in teaching your young pup to sit every time you stop. I much prefer the Stand. This is easier on a young developing pup with lots of heavy bone who would be worn out from all that up and down. The Stand is a valuable command for the breed ring as well, so why not! With your pup heeling happily at your side simply take a few slowing steps to signal a change is coming. Sing out her name and the Stand command, and at the same time release the lead (which is also held by your right hand) with your left hand. Reach down slowly with your left hand and quietly slip your hand in behind her front legs just in front of the stifle. Praise for this (as a treat is impossible to get to), and go right on with your heeling routine. After you sense she is getting the idea, stop and let her stand for a few seconds while you dig out a treat. If she is still standing, give a treat and make a big fuss. If she sits or jumps around, gently guide her back into the Stand and reward with a treat immediately. Don't dwell on how long it took, just move on.

When your pup begins to stand on her own whenever you stop, you may begin finishing your exercises for that day by teaching the Stay. Since the Stay means "Stay here until I return to you," do not ask her to come or sit or anything else from this command. That is the reason for finishing your exercises with it. As with the Sit-Stay, sing out her name and the command "Stay," and back away from her in a standing position. At first you will simply stand in front of her, but as she becomes steadier you will go farther away until you have let out all of the leash and are standing at the end. This will take many sessions and you must continue to lavish the rewards even if your dog only "stays" for a few seconds. Since you are finishing your exercises with this command, make it fun. Keep it up and move quickly through the exercises each day. One success in each area is enough when you are training a very young pup up to four months of age. If you are training an older dog you can repeat the exercises more often. Dogs get bored just as people do so don't plod through it. Keep it exciting and fun, fun, fun.

When you have mastered the Stand-Stay, have a family member or friend walk up to the dog and, at first, just run a hand down the dog's back and walk away while you steady her. If she remains standing during this, reward with a treat! If she doesn't, run through it until you get an improved response, and reward that. Work up to this slowly. It is important that your dog Stand for Examination if you plan to show in Obedience competition. But it is also useful in the conformation ring as well as at home for parasite examination and treatment by a veterinarian.

THE DOWN AND STAY

The Down is often the most difficult command to teach a Bernese Mountain Dog. This is the ultimate act of submission, short

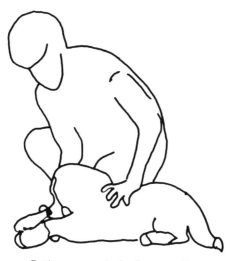

Putting a puppy in the Down position

Returning to the Sit position from the Down

of turning belly-up to expose herself. Introduce the Down as softly and as easily as you can and don't become frustrated. Your sweet pup may suddenly become a wild beast rather than submit. Take it slow. If she gets it right, have a treat handy even if you have to hold it between your teeth! If at all possible teach this to a young pup. It is physically much easier with a lightweight—but it can be accomplished with an adult. To teach the Down have your pup sit in the Heel position on your left side. Squat down next to her and pet her. Place your left hand on her shoulders, sing out her name and the Down command. Gently pull her feet out in front with your right hand until she is lying down. When she is lying down give a treat and let go of all restraints. Should she continue in the Down position, reward again. If you had a struggle, let her up after the treat and go on with other lessons, but return to this one at the end of your session. Save up treats to lavish on her for getting this one right even if only for a second. The next day start with the Down. Give her a second to get it on her own for a treat. But if she doesn't, swiftly put her in the Down, give a treat and move on. Never dwell on a bad experience or a battle. As before, always act as if you knew she would eventually get it right. She will take clues from you, the pack leader, and her self-confidence will go sky-high along with yours—positive, positive!

To vary your routine have your pup Down after the Come, rather than sit. After she does this you can return her to the Sit and finish from that Sit position. To return to the Sit from a Down, when the pup is lying in front of you sing out her name, "Sit" and brush your foot between her front feet. Her reaction will be to back up into the Sit position. You can now use your "finish" or Heel command to bring her around to the Heel position and continue with your exercises.

The Stay is the same for the Down as the Sit and Stand. Slowly build up the time in the down, add the Stay command and begin working your way slowly out to the end of the leash.

TREATS FOR TRAINING

If you are having a hard time with the right treats for training you might try the following liver cookie recipe. This is also good for the show ring, but sometimes a bit dry. In the show ring dogs are trotting around over and over again and plain baked liver is more moist and less likely to encourage panting. But liver cookies are ideal for home and obedience class training.

Liver Cookies

 1 cup corn meal
 1 cup flour
 1 pound raw liver
 1 or 2 cloves garlic

Put all ingredients in a food processor and blend well. Spray a little vegetable oil on a cookie sheet and spread the mixture about one-quarter inch thick. Bake at 400 degrees for 12–15 minutes or until it is firm to the touch. Remove from oven, cool and cut into 1″ × 2″ squares. Use some for training and store the rest in a container in the freezer. Remove a handful a few minutes before training or defrost in your pocket on the way to class.

I suggest that you not use hot dogs or wieners for training. They are full of nitrites that are suspected of causing cancer. If your dog likes broccoli or carrots, apples or oranges, by all means use them, just steer clear of problem foods. If it's not good for you, it's probably not good for your dog either.

TRAINING THE RETRIEVE

This begins by teaching your Bernese to hold something in her mouth. I use the command "Take it"—you can use whatever command works for you. Call your dog in an up, happy voice. When she comes, wagging, happy and hopefully panting just a little, simply say "Take it" and drop the glove in her open mouth while your free hand holds under her chin so she must continue to hold the glove. (She must lower her head or open her mouth to drop it.) Walk around praising her and telling her how brilliant she is. Then take your hand away and with your other hand grasp the glove and remove it from her mouth using any appropriate command such as "Out"—just continue to use the same command. Continue to do this two or three times a day. Make it a fun game. Do not remove your hand and allow her to the drop the glove. Encourage success, not failure! When you think your Berner has the idea, try letting go of her lower jaw only for a moment or two and asking her to bring you the glove. Running backward will encourage her to follow just as it did when you were teaching her to come. Use your Come command and keep your eye on her. If she looks like she is ready to drop the glove, take it from her, while commanding "Out" or "Release," and praise her as if that was what she intended. Take the glove, reward with food and let this be the end of the session—always end on a happy note. As soon as you feel she is comfortable and steady with taking something and holding it until you give the command to release or "Out," you may begin training her to retrieve from the ground. Place the glove on the ground, point to it and give the same command you have been using for her to take it from your hand. Example: "Bernice, Take it." Should she not get the idea, pick it up and place it in her mouth and go back to your original training practice of holding her chin. Keep a positive attitude and lots of up, happy praise. What you say is not as encouraging as how you say it. If the tail is wagging, your tone of voice is right! If your dog is slow to learn, alternate praise and food. Ignore her mistakes, encourage her successes. I would not resort to using the force-retrieve method of training on a Bernese. You may end up with a dog that will stubbornly refuse to ever retrieve anything and will never forgive you, no matter how much water passes under the bridge.

SHOWING IN OBEDIENCE

Should your training lead you to believe that your dog has a real aptitude for obedience you may decide to take it one step further and get her ready for formal Obedience competition. The best way to accomplish this is by joining a training class. Your dog will become familiar with working in the midst of other dogs and you will be taught the Obedience ring procedure or what is expected of you in an actual Obedience Trial. These classes are often given by local all-breed clubs and may have different levels of instruction. A local fancier, your vet or an animal control officer can direct you to a class near you. If your pup is performing all of the exercises

Ch. Broken Oaks Arjana, CD, owned, bred and handled by Gale Werth, was accomplished as a winner and a producer and excelled in obedience competition—truly a versatile, well-rounded dog that was a credit to the breed.

Gruezli Etain, Am., Can. CDX, TD, owned by Linda Foti, combines grace and strength as he effortlessly clears the broad jump.

we have discussed, you will be ready for the second level of instruction. You will be working off lead some of the time, but don't be afraid to put your dog back on lead anytime you feel it is necessary. Take your food with you and your buckle collar. If the class turns into one of the usual jerk-correction classes, follow along, but use your method, not the jerk. Stay with your up, chirpy, quick work, no matter how foolish you feel. When the other class members see how happy your dog is, they may even switch to your method. Don't be goaded into doing it their way. If push comes to shove and the instructor insists on compliance, ask for your money back and enroll in another class. The best way to pick a class is to go and observe. Even if you must sit through a whole series of training sessions you will still be learning and not subjecting your dog to a potentially unpleasant experience. Don't join an obedience class during the adolescent period, it is a waste of time. Wait until this period is over. Do join in the thirteenth week right after your home training course. Just partake in the class until you see the pup tiring, then retire to the sidelines and watch. Your pup is now ready for the more formal training and mild corrections.

LIFE AFTER OBEDIENCE TRAINING

Now what? You've opened up the lines of communication with your dog, you've finished obedience classes and perhaps formal Obedience Trials don't really appeal to you. You'd rather just have fun with your dog! Well, you are in luck! There are many new avenues to pursue with your newfound skills. Agility is one of the highest spirited. This involves training your dog to literally run through a course of obstacles during which time she can demonstrate her agility. The dogs and owners alike love this sport and is it ever fun!

Another terrific fun sport is Flyball. This is a team sport in which the teams take turns racing their dogs over a series of hurdles to a box at the end of the course. The box has a lever that the dog jumps on to release a ball which it catches and returns over the

The winners of Team Obedience at the 1993 BMDCA line up for whimsical win picture to record their achievement.

Agility is a fairly recent wrinkle in sport with dogs. It is exciting and involving as these photos show and is gaining in popularity every day.

hurdles to its waiting handler. This sport is very exciting and usually draws a very enthusiastic crowd. Hurdle racing is very similar, and is also a team sport. Lastly, there is team obedience. This sport can bring out some pretty unusual teams that all just want to have fun, not unlike their fun-loving dogs!

SIGNIFICANT BERNESE IN OBEDIENCE

The First Obedience Title Holders

The first Bernese to earn the Companion Dog title was Aya of Verlap (Sire: Banz v. d. Kuhweid, Dam: Lory v. Sunnehuebeli), bred by Nelly Frey and owned by Mary Alice Horstick (Eschweiler) and W. W. Horstick. The year was 1962. The first Bernese to earn a Companion Dog Excellent degree was Wilhelmina v. Neugebauer, owned by Hugh O'Hagan. She annexed the title in 1972 and the first Utility Bernese was Ch. Dina de L'Armary (Sire: Jumbo de Bottassiaux, Dam: Juta V. Rappenfluh), bred by Jean Badertacher and owned by Mary Alice Horstick (Eschweiler).

High Scoring Dogs by Year

Year	Dog/Owner(s)	Class	Avg. Score
1974	William Tell v. Wyemede, CD Owner/Ruth & Thomas Howard	Novice	N/A
1975	Dina de L'Armary, CD Owner/Mary Alice Horstick (Eschweiler)	Novice	N/A
1976	Ch. Mon Plaisir's Shady Lady, CD Owner/Gale Werth	Novice	193.16
	Ch. Dina de L'Armary, CDX Owner/Mary Alice Horstick (Eschweiler)	Open	188.3
1977	Franklin Farm's Ophelia, CD Owner/Kathy Sartor & David Andrews	Novice	192.5

Year	Dog/Owner(s)	Class	Avg. Score
	Ch. Mon Plaisir's Shady Lady, CDX	Open	190.7
1978	Broken Oaks Arjana, CD Owner/Gale Werth	Novice B	194.7
	Contessa di Montagna Owner/Peg Forte	Open	186
1979	Wyemede's Mountainside Max, CD Owner/Louis & Bonnie Koncz	Novice A	193.5
	Ch. Alphorn's Humeresque, CDX Owner/Linda Williams	Open	192
	Ch. Dina de L'Armary, UD Owner/Mary Alice Horstick (Eschweiler)	Utility	190.8
1980	Ch. Broken Oaks Bergita, CD, TD Owner/Andrew & Margie Reho	Novice	195.5
	Ch. Dagne v. Hexliheim, CDX Owner/Mary Alice Horstick (Eschweiler)	Open A	187.3
1981	Ch. Andre v. Monaco, CD Owner/Larry Flexer	Novice	196.4
	Bernfield's Astrea v. Car Mar, CDX Owner/April Rifenburg	Open	193
1982	Andare Bene Barli Noir Owner/Margaret & Leslie Baird	Novice	194.8
	Byrnwood's Alpen Lupine, CDX Owner/Agnes Kinsella	Open	195.17
1983	Ch. Mt. Mist Halidom Mindy v. Davos, CD Owner/Millicent Parliman & Barbara Salamun	Novice	191.2
	Larissa v. d. Beernau Owner/Heidy & W. N. Naegeli	Open A	190.5

Year	Dog/Owner(s)	Class	Avg. Score
	Kaylin's Bridget Bardot, CDX Owner/Dorothy Lademann & Linda Williams	Open B	192
	Ch. Felicidae's Calypso of Aspen, UTD Owner/Kenneth & Phyllis Collier	Utility	187.17
1984	Dallybeck's Anneke v. Ashley, CD Owner/Andrew & Marjorie Reho	Novice	194.2
	The Chaletsuizo's Fleur, CDX Owner/David & Coral Denis	Open A	180.2
1985	Ch. Shepard's Patch Elise, CD, TD Owner/Mary Alice Eschweiler	Novice B	191.33
	Nordstaaten's Emma, CDX Owner/Ruth Ballmer	Open A	192.7
	Bernfeild's Astrea v. Car-Mar, UD Owner/April & Ervin Rifenburg	Utility	189.7
1986	Moonshadow's Nighttime Mika, CD Owner/Anne Nichols	Novice	194.33
	Ch. Kemahtrail's Brekke, CDX Owner/Katherine Miller & Janice Lebeuf	Open A	194.83
	Ch. Dallybeck's Destry, CDX Owner/Bill Hammer	Open B	189.38
1987	Ch. Arundel's Star Caper, CDX Owner/Paula Hopkins	Novice	195.17
	Ch. Arundel's Star Caper, CDX Owner/Paula Hopkins	Open A	197.16
	Ch. Kemahtrail's Brekke, CDX Owner/Katherine Miller & Janice Lebeuf	Open B	194.3
	Ch. Shersan Brite N Shining Star, UD Owner/Jerry Hughes	Utility	195

High Scoring Dogs by Year (*cont.*)

Year	Dog/Owner(s)	Class	Avg. Score
1988	Ch. Bev's Star Buck v. Mi-Ja's, CD Owner/Mary Jane & Michael Mielke	Novice	196
	Sandusky's Mutadis Mutandis, CDX Owner/Kathleen Galotti & Lloyd Komatsu	Open A	188.5
	Ch. Arundel's Star Caper, CDX Owner/Paula Hopkins	Open B	195.16
	Ch. Kemahtrail's Brekke, CDX Owner/Katherine Miller & Janice Lebeuf	Utility	186.66
1989	Sandusky's Brighteye Abigail, CD, TD Owner/Deborah Hotze	Novice	196.6
	Weyrbern's Grande Damia, CDX, TD Owner/Katherine & Christopher Milar	Open A	194.5
	Sandusky's Brighteye Abigail, CD, TD Owner/Deborah Hotze	Open B	195.5
	Rif's Turbo Charger, UDT Owner/April Rifenburg	Utility	181
1990	Halidom Chelsea v. Dante, CD Owner/Louise Wetzel	Novice A	190.8
	Brighteye Nelle Belle, CD, TD Owner/Deborah Hotze	Novice B	198
	Ahquabi's Raven v. Bauernhof, CDX, TD Owner/Kathy Berge	Open A	192.7
	Sandusky's Mutadis Mutandis, CDX Owner/Kathleen Galotti & Lloyd Komatsu	Open B	192
	Ch. Arundel's Star Caper, CDX Owner/Paula Hopkins	Utility	194.7

High Scoring Dogs by Year (*cont.*)

Year	Dog/Owner(s)	Class	Avg. Score
1991	Greenway's Piper Heidsick, CD Owner/Dierdre Laveran	Novice A	192
	Ch. Random's Kalista, CD Owner/Dr. Patricia Losco	Novice B	191.8
	Gunnison Von Speicher, CDX Owner/Fred & Margaret Bartell	Open A	193.8
	Sandusky's Ceteris Paribus, CDX Owner/Lloyd Komatsu & Kathleen Galotti	Open B	192.1
	Sandusky's Mutadis Mutandis, UD Owner/Kathleen Galotti & Lloyd Komatsu	Utility	187.8
1992	Bornedale's El Oso Grande, CD Owner/Cindi & Ray Rodman	Novice A	191.8
	Liskarn American Bound Jerry, CD, DD Owner/Sara Dombroski, Alison Jaskiewicz & Deborah Mulvey	Novice B	197.3
	Nashems Colorado Rocky, CDX Owner/Cynthia Still	Open A	193.2
	Brighteye Nelle Belle, CD, TD Owner/Deborah Hotze	Novice B	194.8
	Sandusky's Mutadis Mutandis, UD Owner/Kathleen Galotti & Lloyd Komatsu	Utility B	188.7
1993	Ch. Arthos Von Dorneckerberg, CD Owner/Jolie & Martin Kaufmann- Laker	Novice A	191.8
	Ch. Nighttime's Carry-On Kyla Moon, CD Owner/Anne Nichols	Novice B	197.2
	Ch. Swiss Star's Nitro Whatagas, CDX, TDX Owner/April Rifenburg	Open A	191.2

Year	Dog/Owner(s)	Class	Avg. Score
	Random's Rabble Rouser, UD Owner/Patricia Losco No Utility B in 1993	Utility A	184.2

Top Producers of Obedience Title Holders
Sires—Cumulative

# Titles	Name of Sire (Studbook Issue)	Owner/Breeder
19	Ch. Halidom Davos v. Yodlerhof, CD (5/77)	Buchanan-Parliman/Brooks
16	Ch. Jaycy's Wyatt Vom Hund See (12/84)	Burney/Rutter
14	Ch. Ashley v. Bernerliebe (11/80)	Ohlsen/Ohlsen
11	Ch. Pike's Chewbacca (9/80)	Kara/Pike
11	Ch. Wyemede Luron Bruce (5/79)	Buss/Crawford
10	Ch. Ami v. d. Swisstop Farms (5/82) (Can.)	Townsend/Schaer (Can.)
10	Ch. De-Li's Foreign Touch (1/88)	Ostermiller/Ostermiller
9	Ch. Argon v. Wil-Lancer (7/72)	Reisinger/O'Hagan
9	Ch. Bauernhofs Bear Paws (9/80)	Shambeau/Kelley
9	Ch. Bev's Baron v. Greybern (5/88)	Burney/Gray
9	Nova Polaris (9/82)	Shambeau/Pike
8	Ch. Deer Park Heartlight (5/85)	Dean/Curtis & Dean
7	Can. Ch. Bari Von Nydegghoger (8/82)	Smith/Stockli (Switz.)

Top Producers of Obedience Title Holders (*cont.*)
Sires—Cumulative

# Titles	Name of Sire (Studbook Issue)	Owner/Breeder
7	Ch. Klaus v. Buchsischlossli (8/82)	Russ/Sollberger
7	Ch. Kuster's Jocko Of J Bar (4/76)	Kuster & Johnson/Alpstein Kennel
7	Ch. Olly Von Tonisbach (5/84)	Guido/Schaffer (Switz.)
7	Ch. Shersan's Black Tie Required (8/86)	Kinley/Kinley
6	Ch. Alex Von Weissenburg (11/85)	Donohew/Schofer (Switz.)
6	Ch. Alphorn's Copyright v. Echo (3/77)	Johnson/Johnson
6	Ch. Donar v. Mutschen (10/88)	Hauser/Schrode (Switz.)
6	Ch. Jaycy's Uri Vom Hund See (12/83)	Burney/Rutter
6	Ch. Jean Henry La Vaux, CD, TD (2/76)	Horstick (Eschweiler)/ Meister (Switz.)
6	Mt. Chalet's Epic v. Lancer (10/72)	Pyle/Pyle
6	Rambo v. d. Schwarzwasserfluh (10/87)	Reufenacht/Zbinden (Switz.)
6	Ch. Santera Rio Grando v. Crest (9/88)	Novocin/Novocin
6	Ch. Shepherd's Patch Czar Wyemede, CD (2/82)	Crawford/Horstick (Eschweiler)
6	Ch. Wunderstrand's Arlac v. Chavanne, CD (2/81)	Barney/Fawer (Can.)

Top Producers of Obedience Title Holders
Dams—Cumulative

# Titles	Name of Dam (Studbook Issue)	Owner/Breeder
8	Ch. Sandusky's Brighteye Abigail, UDT (1/89)	Hotze/Ongemach
6	Ch. Bev's Jabbering Jodi V, BB (8/84)	Burney/Burney
6	Ch. Gretchen Von Woener, CD (9/80)	Woerner & Ongemach/ Kelley
6	Ch. Merrimac Mijay's Black Label, CDX (9/86)	Walker/Mahaffey
6	Ch. Trilogy's Torch Of Snowmont (12/86)	Cummings/Tramp
5	Ch. Broken Oaks Bergita, CDX, TD (10/81)	Reho/Werth
5	Ch. Dagne v. Hexliheim, CDX (5/79)	Horstick (Eschweiler)/ Dawson
5	Ch. Dallybeck's Cresta v. Bergita, CD (3/87)	Reho/Reho
5	Ch. Mon Plaisir's Shady Lady, CDX (3/77)	Werth/Gagnon
5	Ch. Sandusky's My Name Is Helga, CDX (9/86)	Ongemach/Ongemach & Shambeau
4	Bauernhof's Rika Von Davos (6/81)	Barney/Kelley
4	Ch. Broken Oaks Arjana, CD (4/80)	Werth/Werth
4	Ch. Broken Oaks Butik, CD (3/82)	Werth/Werth
4	Ch. DeerPark Ferkin v. Buttonwillow (4/84)	Dean/Russ
4	Ch. Dina De L'Armary, UDT (7/77) (Switz.)	Horstick/Badertacher
4	Ch. Guezi Patty Melt v. Reuben, CD (4/88)	Getzel/Getzel
4	Mt. View's Mademoiselle Marie, CD (10/87)	Peters/Edwards

Top Producers of Obedience Title Holders (*cont.*)
Dams—Cumulative

# Titles	Name of Dam (Studbook Issue)	Owner/Breeder
4	Ch. Oberland Elian v. Bernerliebe (10/84)	Roth/Goodman & Ohlsen
4	Sanctuary Woods Color Scheme (7/69)	Pyle/Knight
4	Ch. Shepard's Patch Dionne, CD (11/83)	Evert & Eschweiler/ Horstick
4	Ch. Stassi's Elka Sommer Schoen, CD (10/79)	Sommers/Pennington
4	Ch. Sunnyhill's Anna v. Jimco (10/75)	Kullman/Cotter
4	Ch. Tanja v. Nesselacker, CD, TD (5/75) (Switz.)	Gruber/Krauchi (Switz.)
4	Ch. Texas Tiffany Vombreiterweg, CDX (7/79)	Tramp/Townsend
4	Ch. Tonia v. Barenried (2/86) (Switz.)	Ostermiller/Jsch

Bernese Mountain Dog Club of America National Specialty High in Trials

Year	Dog	Owner/Breeder
1976	HIT Mon Plaisir's Executive Touch	Alan & Karen Farkas
1977	HIT Mt. Chalet's Unique v. Epic	Robert & Margaret Lentz
1978	HIT Broken Oaks Arjana	Gale Werth/owner
1979	HIT Taliesin Copy v. Meadowrock	D. Currie/Brenda Abrams
1980	HIT Bernfield's Astrea v. Car-Mar	April & Ervin Rifenburg/ D. & G. Tribukait
1981	HIT Kaylin's Brigette Bardot	Dorothy Lademan & Linda Williams/Linda Williams

Bernese Mountain Dog Club of America National Specialty High in Trials (*cont.*)

Year	Dog	Owner/Breeder
1982	HIT Andare Bere Bahi Noir	Leslie & Margaret Baird/ Martha Reisinger
1983	HIT Bernfield's Astrea v. Car-Mar, CDX	April & Ervin Rifenburg/ D. & G. Tribukait
1984	HIT Walchwil Robin Hood	Kathleen Rundquist/Mr. & Mrs. G. Howard
1985	HIT Dallybeck's Andrea Bella	Marjorie Reho/Andrew & Marjorie Reho
1989	HIT Bernfield's Astrea v. Car-Mar, UDT	April & Ervin Rifenburg/ D. & G. Tribukait
1987	HIT Ch. Greuzi Patty Melt v. Reuben	Krista, Ardene & Walter Getzel/Krista & Ardene Getzel
1988	HIT Sandusky's Brighteye Abigail	Deborah Hotze/Sandra Ongemach
1989	HIT Zeder Hugle's Raleigh v. Rolo, CD	Ruth Prenosil/Jack Klassen
1990	HIT Brighteye Nelle Belle, TD	Deborah Hotze/owner
1991	HIT Ch. Zeder Hugle's Raleigh v. Rolo, CDX	Ruth Prenosil/Jack Klassen
1992	HIT Ch. Swiss Star's Nitro Whatagas, TD	April Rifenburg/Barbara & William Hefner
1993	HIT Felicidads Brighteye Anabel, U-CD, CGC, Can. CD	Glenn & Debbie Holtze/ Phyllis Collier
1994	HIT Windy Knob's Finishing Touch	Jerry Hughes/J. Hughes

6

Tracking

DO BERNESE have the required natural instincts to make them good tracking dogs? The following quote from Dr. Scheidegger, as related by Dr. Albert Heim, in the early 1900's would certainly suggest they do.

> Rosi von Burdorf (S.H.S.B. 4545) was sent by train on a rainy day to a new owner in a distant town about eight hours away. After several days she was released from a chain at 8:00 A.M. in dull rainy weather. She had never before been in that region. At 4:00 P.M. she appeared at her old home. Such carrier pigeon–like work would make a trained police dog honored.

This quote also gives us a little insight into the basics of tracking. First, a dog can distinguish between scents, and will not lose a weaker scent among heavier ones. So Rosi was able to find the way home even though it was and had been raining for several days. The second principle is that a dog can follow airborne scents as well as ground scents over almost any terrain. Thus Rosi was able to pick up the scent even though she had been transported by train, for there is no way she could have seen where she was going or could have remembered the route. Lastly, a dog follows a trail

Ch. Tanja v. Nesselacker (Graf v. Barenried ex Miggi v. Nesselacker), owned and handled by Max Gruber, was the first Bernese Mountain Dog to earn a Tracking degree. This milestone was achieved in 1976.

in his own way that is unique to him alone. In this last manner Rosi would have astonished even a trained tracking dog.

Bernese can track, some better than others, as with most working dogs. A few things will have to be added to your basic obedience skills if you want to compete in AKC tracking trials and earn a TD, most noticeably, retrieving. Tracking is a natural instinct that you perfect in your dog and bring out, not something that you train. You will work with your dog in the beginning, guiding him toward what he already knows how to do. Therefore, it is very important that you study and observe his every move and body signal so you will later understand him and his way of tracking. This will help you guide him toward your mutual goal, the article at the end of

174

the track! When training, remember Rosi and ask yourself if you could find your way eight hours from home from a trip where you couldn't see where you were going. This will help you to respect the awesome powers of a Bernese Mountain Dog's nose, and keep you from trying to outsniff your dog!

BASIC TRACKING EQUIPMENT

The equipment used in tracking can have double use; your carting harness can double as a tracking harness and vice versa, so look for one you can adapt for both. The harness is the best way to pick up on your dog's body signals, as sometimes you may be working up to thirty feet away from your dog. You will also quickly progress to needing a thirty-foot lead. Some old clothesline can do nicely until you decide if tracking is your thing. Don't get brilliant and use your Flexi-lead as the handle leaves you out of touch with your dog's body language. It's like driving a station wagon instead of a sports car—you just can't feel the road. Lastly, you will need some stakes so you can mark the beginning and end of the track. These are guideposts so *you* know were the track is; your dog doesn't need them. At the end of each track there should be an article—an old gardening glove is handy for this, particularly one of leather or suede. Bernese seem to find these materials the most appealing. This is important, for soon they will have to retrieve them.

BASIC TRAINING

To begin tracking, your Berner will need the basic obedience skills learned in Chapter 5. If you are one of the lucky few with a Bernese who is a natural retriever you may begin training with the retrieving game. Put your dog on a Sit-Stay. Walk out about twenty feet, shake the glove so he will see it, drop it, return to your dog and send him out to retrieve it. After your dog plays the game a few times and gets terribly excited after he finds the glove and brings it back, you can progress to hiding the article behind a building and making him use his nose to find it.

This simple training gives him the idea of moving forward and searching out an article. If you are one of the rest of the Bernese owners in this world with a Berner who thinks retrieving is stupid, your early training program will start out with laying a short track in a field that is not highly contaminated with other scents. A few other scents are to be expected; just avoid a well-traveled public area. Start out using stakes to define your track at each end, so you will know exactly were the track is, enabling you to point it out to your Berner.

Some of the same rules governing early obedience training also apply: eliminate distractions and keep it simple. Laying your track in a low traffic area keeps the scent you want your dog to follow stronger with fewer competing scents. Thus, you are eliminating distractions. You are keeping it simple by retracing your track in plain sight of your dog. After you have layed your track, bring your dog to the beginning of the track, leave him on a Sit-Stay, follow your track to the end, make a fuss and let him see the article. Drop the article and return to your dog, rewalking your track. Begin your training by taking your dog on a six-foot lead to the beginning of the track, point to the ground and ask him to "Find it" or any other expression that will mean "try this" to him. The commands are up to you, just make it fun and happy. The minute you feel he is getting the idea by sniffing and moving out, give lots of praise and encouragement.

Communication is the only tool you have to bring out your dog's natural instincts. They cannot be forced, only nurtured. If your Berner takes to tracking like he was born to it, you can modify some of the encouragement. A natural tracker often finds too much talk distracting and it can break his concentration. Once your dog begins to follow the track just walk along with him, keeping the lead taught; if he wanders too far astray calmly direct him back to the track with your lead, point to the track and encourage to continue. When he finally makes it to the last stake and finds the article, praise him lavishly, with even more enthusiasm than you've been using to encourage him on the track. As you continue your training and begin to work longer straight tracks, you should be aware of the presence of airborne or wind scent. Wind scent is deposited on high objects such as trees and shrubs as well as in low areas such as ditches and gullies. Your dog may often follow these wind scents as well as the ground scent. Don't conclude he is no longer on the track should he begin to zigzag back and forth or sniff at the air. This is an area where your dog knows more than you do. You must learn to trust your dog and try not to second-guess him. Observe him carefully and commit his body signals and style of tracking to memory so you will be confident of his purpose in a tracking test where you will be following a blind track with only your dog to guide you. Continue to work your straight track, extending its length and the length of lead you extend for the dog to work on. Bernese naturally pull in a harness so it should be easy to convince your dog to pull you forward on the track. Let out just enough lead to keep the line taught while your Berner works, and always keep up the words of encouragement. Your early training should be conducted on a fresh track of up to fifteen minutes old. When your dog is comfortable working out in front of you on a taught line following a straight track of 100 to 150 feet, and you are confident in his ability, you may progress to:

1. Adding turns (always using a stake at the turn) of 90 degrees and only 90 degrees. Should you see the dog forging well beyond the stake turn, simply hold your ground and stand still, taking up or letting out line as needed until your dog finds the scent has turned. As soon as he picks up the scent and turns, give lots of praise and encouragement. Should he lose the scent and not know where to look, guide him in the direction of the turn with the lead and encourage him to hunt for the scent. Your communication skills in this area should be very well developed by now, enabling him to understand your words of encouragement. Only resort to this guidance after you have given him ample opportunity to pick up the scent on his own; he is the real expert here.

2. Work your way up to older tracks. Start with your fifteen-minute track and add fifteen-minute increments until you are working on tracks that are two hours old.

3. Have another person lay your track and plant the article(s). Select for your track layer someone who will defer to your judgment or someone who is familiar with tracking and track laying.

4. Seek out many types of weather conditions in which to work. Rain, fog, humidity, sunshine, all make for good

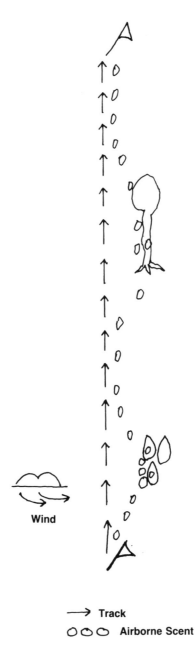

Wind

→ Track

◯◖◗ Airborne Scent

The dog may leave the track briefly to follow airborne scent and then return to the original track.

A typical example of a straight track approximately fifty feet long.

experiences. This is something you will have no control over in a tracking trial, so by training under all these conditions you will know how to read your dog in any situation.

BAITING THE TRACK

Remember the old fable of Hansel and Gretel, whose wicked stepfather led them off into the woods, and Hansel, uneasy about the whole thing, left a trail of bread crumbs behind? We all remember that the birds ate all the crumbs, leaving the children stranded in the woods. Baiting the track can leave you stranded as well. Your dog may do it only for the bread crumbs and never for a track! So only use this method as a last resort when you have exhausted all other possibilities. Some stubborn Berners cannot be encouraged by any other method. The usual method is to deprive the dog of food for a day, not usually necessary with Bernese—the way to a Bernese Mountain Dog's brain is most often through its stomach. Lay out your track with stakes as before, keep it fairly short and leave a trail of goodies on the track, with the largest treat at the end. Slowly eliminate every other piece of food until you have very few treats along the way, and give lots of encouragement whenever your dog is sniffing the trail, not when he is eating the treats—they are encouragement enough. Always begin by pointing to the ground and telling him ''Find it,'' or ''Track,'' or whatever command communicates the idea to him. As you lengthen the distances between morsels at each training session, observe your dog's behavior carefully. Eventually you will eliminate the bait and only use it to reward him when he finds the article at the end of the trail. Hopefully he will pick up on the idea of tracking from this encouragement and prefer the track to the bait. But only you, with lots of praise and reward for his successes, can make tracking more rewarding than food.

PREPARING FOR THE TD

The goal of all this training is, for some, simply the pleasure of working with their dog as a team. For others it may be to develop another skill in the beloved family pet that may be useful someday (such as tracking and recovering a lost person), but for many it is to achieve the coveted title of TD (Tracking Degree). If this is your goal, the best way to learn what is expected of you at a tracking trial is to attend several trials as an observer. For the current test rules as well as a judge's guide, write to the American Kennel Club, 51 Madison Ave., New York, N.Y. 10010, and request a copy of the tracking regulations.

Tracking Dogs

Year	Dog	Owner
1976	Ch. Tanja v. Nesselacker, CD, bitch	Max Gruber
1977	Sablemate Beautiful Dream, CD, dog	Katherine Kwiatkowski
	Chesebek's Beryl v. Bernerbear, bitch	Ed & Barbara Rice
1978	Am., Can. Ch. Sunnyhill's Helga v. Ulrica, CD, bitch	Beverly Barney
1979	Maren's Zuckerplatzchen, CD, bitch	Jane McGovern
	Ch. Martha's Teddy Bear, CD, bitch	Sam & Martha Decker
	Sablemate Esprit de Vie, bitch	John H. Thompson, Jr.
	Ch. Wyemede 'N Palmer ''B'' Bernerbear	Gail Palmer
	Felicidad's Calypso of Aspin, bitch	Kenneth W. Collier & Elizabeth Farnum
1980	Ch. Jean Henri la Vaux, CD, dog	Mary Alice Horstick
	Ch. Broken Oaks Bergita, bitch	Andrew & Marjorie Reho
1981	Ch. Bernbrae's Alm Lucienne, bitch	Jane McGovern
	Ch. Dina de l'Armary, UD, bitch	Mary Alice Horstick
1982	Maren's Yosemite Sam v. Blass, CDX, dog	George Coulter

Tracking Dogs (*cont.*)

Year	Dog	Owner
	Bernerhaus Ona Lee v. Mt. Chalet, CDX, bitch	M. E. Packard & T. E. Likins
	Elka's Brie of Kemahtrail, CDX, bitch	C. R. & K. S. Milar
	Yogi v.d. Berghen Weide, dog	Loes de Ruyter
1983	Ch. Fexen v. Felstal, CDX, dog	K. M. Higgins & J. C. Turner
1984	Bauernhof's Fancy Free, bitch	Martha Decker
	Wyemede's Aquila v. Butik, bitch	Peg Forte & S. D'Ambola
	Beowoof of Sunnyhill, dog	L. Packard
	Viva's Graemlicher Bischof, dog	C. Gramlich
	Shepherd's Patch Abigail, bitch	M. A. Eschweiler
1985	Kuni v. Nordstaaten, CD, dog	M. E. & B. G. Packard
	Ch. Shepherd's Patch Elise, bitch	M. A. Horstick Eschweiler
	Weyrbern's Grande Damia, bitch	K. S. & C. R. Milar
1986	Bernfleid's Astrea v. Car-Mar, UD, bitch	A. & E. Rifenburg
1987	Geneva von Herbst, CD, bitch	C. C. & E. A. Palmer
	Bauernhof's Fancy Free, CD, bitch	M. Decker
	Sandusky's Brighteye Abigail, bitch	D. Hotze
1988	Sandusky's Timely Tabitha, CD, bitch	M. E. & C. L. Bond
	Rif's Turbo Charger, CDX, dog	A. Rifenburg

Year	Dog	Owner
	Durbach Bravo Ziggy Stardust, dog	B. Sanders
	Ch. Olympians Oracle of Delphi, CD, bitch	A. Jaskiewicz & E. Brouck
	Rockies Aura of Brighteye, bitch	D. S. Hotze
	Taliesin's Marney-B, bitch	E. H. Nott
1990	Brighteye Nelle Belle, bitch	D. S. Hotze
	Rockie's Aspenhund Heidil, CD, bitch	J. H. Shaw
	Gruezi's Noble Nanny, CD, bitch	G. B. Simcoe
	Brighteye Lucy v. Friichnicht, bitch	D. S. Hotze
	Ahquabi's Raven von Bauernhof, CDX, bitch	K. Berge
	Ch. Zeder Hugel's Raleigh v. Rolo, CDX, dog	R. Prenosil
1991	Ch. Sandusky's Patton Vahn Eli, dog	R. L. Cozzolino
	Magic Mountain v. Bernerliebe, CDX, bitch	M. Rosner
	Seacrest-Bev's Raven v. Random, CDX, bitch	P. E. Losco
	Skye Tylor Vombreiterweg, dog	C. & E. Smith
	Alpenrose Mis-T-Magic Spirit, bitch	L. Kelley & S. Hostetter
1992	Ch. Swiss Stars Nitro Whatagas, dog	A. Rifenburg
1993	Brighteyed Molly McGee, bitch	D. S. Hotze
	Ch. Brighteye Clancy O'Creekwood	M. & C. Bond

Tracking Dogs Excellent

Year	Dog	Owner
1985	Viva's Graemlicher Bischof, TD, dog	C. Gramlich
1988	Sandusky's Timely Tabitha, CD, TD, bitch	M. E. Dods & C. L. Bond
1991	Durbach Bravo Ziggy Stardust, TD, dog	B. Sanders
1993	Ch. Swiss Stars Nitro Whatagas, CD, TD, dog	A. Rifenburg

7

Carting

How PICTURESQUE it must have been in Switzerland, in days gone by, to see the once-familiar draft dog in harness working alongside a farmer, baker or even a postman. Bernese Mountain Dogs are rumored to have been so self-confident and aloof that they actually took the milk to the dairy alone and returned with the empty milk cans. Most often, however, they were accompanied by the farm children.

They are said to have waited patiently outside the village dairies while their milk cans were emptied. Any growling or grumbling was halted by a shout from within the dairy. The children took turns riding in the carts on the way back home.

In the United States, carting is prohibited in many states—and often well-intentioned people criticize it as a form of animal cruelty. It is actually just the opposite. The Bernese truly loves this activity and all the attention that goes with it.

This is what makes him a member of the Working Group. He was bred for a purpose—draft work and droving. The Bernese Mountain Dog's ability in this area sets him apart from other breeds. Carting brings a Bernese to life, showing an entirely new side to his nature. This is his job! Your carefree clown may suddenly become a purposeful, responsible animal when hooked to a cart.

A charming rendering of present and future carting Berners and the people in their lives from *All Creatures Great and Small*, by Claudia Post Schaffer, copyright 1991. Reprinted with permission.

Carting brings you and your Bernese closer together and makes you a team as nothing else can. So check your local ordinances—especially if you are invited to participate in a public event such as a parade or a play. And start out right with the proper training. Once you have trained your Berner to pull a cart, you will wonder how you ever got along without him "cart-in-tow."

There are so many ways that your dog will become a more useful family member. He or she will wait patiently as you rake leaves to pull them off to the burn pile, in autumn hauling the winter wood to be stacked or just giving the neighborhood kids a ride. Bernese love to work, and unlike obedience, in which they see very little purpose, they find that carting is indeed a useful activity.

Of course every Bernese has his or her own distinct personality. Some dogs are headstrong and, although quite able to pull a cart, are not willing. Others, even though they may want to cart, are unable to do so as they are structurally not suited to the work. And then there are the dogs that just do not have the ability or the attitude. But you'll never know until you try. So give it a try—most Bernese love it!

TRAINING

A little basic obedience gives you a line of communication with your dog and will make the whole process go much smoother. You can begin obedience with puppies at seven to eight weeks old, as a good grasp of Come, Sit, Down, Stand, Stay and Heel will make draft training much easier. Basic draft training can commence quite early in a dog's life, although training with heavy loads should not begin until a Berner is at least one year of age—better yet, two.

Begin draft training by introducing your dog to the harness. (You can assemble your own tiny puppy harness from lightweight cord for very early training.) Let him sniff it and just get used to its presence. Lay it across his back and praise lavishly. Once he decides the harness is a part of his environment, put it on and allow him to go about his normal routine wearing his harness. Do this for a few days in a row for fifteen to twenty minutes a day until he is quite comfortable with the routine of putting the harness on and off and wearing it! Do not leave him unsupervised in harness as a harness can easily become tangled.

When he is thoroughly accustomed to the feel of the harness, attach a couple of ropes and let him drag them around to get used to this sensation. Continue to monitor his activity so he will not become entangled. When your Berner is completely used to the drag of the ropes, which should take about two or three days, you are ready to progress to a lightweight drag. A drag for an adult dog should weigh two or three pounds, and for puppies from eight to ten ounces.

Hook your drag to the lines of your harness, attach a lead to the dog's collar and give him a forward command. Praise highly and talk to him all the while. After a few days, when he has mastered a nice, steady pace, with no galloping or hopping, you are ready to progress to the cart.

This stage is just like the harness—introduce the dog to the cart, let him sniff it, walk him around it and, if possible, leave it somewhere that he will pass often during his daily, supervised routine for a few days. Then begin moving the cart around in your dog's presence, making sure he has no apprehension about the cart before you hitch him to it.

Once he has been carefully introduced, hitch him up to the *empty* cart. Let him see what you are doing at all times. Give lots

Carting is the Bernese Mountain Dog's natural heritage. Training is, therefore, very much a matter of conditioning. This dog is comfortable in the harness, so a drag is attached to accustom the dog to draft work.

The cart should be empty the first time the dog is hitched to it.

of praise and make no sudden movements. Keep him on a leash or have a friend hold his collar so he will not become frightened and run off with the cart doing what he dreads—chasing him! Hook him up and unhook him several days in a row. Before he actually begins pulling the cart, have a friend hold the shafts next to your dog, pretending to be the cart as you hold the collar, walking your dog next to the shaft. Repeat this on his left and right side until he is comfortable with the noise and touch of the shafts.

BASIC CARTING EQUIPMENT

Draft Apparatus

Following are the basic types of apparatus.

1. *Cart*—By definition this is a two-wheeled vehicle, thus it is fairly simple, lightweight and easy to maneuver. The cart is available ready-made or can be built at home. The drawback to a cart is that it has a tendency to tip when loaded improperly.
2. *Wagon*—A four-wheeled vehicle, larger and heavier than a cart, it requires more space to maneuver. Unlike the cart, there is no tipping caused by uneven loads, as the wagon is stable and can easily carry loads as well as people. Although custom dog-size wagons are not readily available, certain types, such as a child's wooden wagon, can be easily converted. (See list of suppliers at the end of this chapter.)
3. *Travois*—Good for bulk loads on rough trails where a cart or wagon cannot go. This Native American type of hauling apparatus has significant drag and may only be used with light loads.
4. *Sled*—Some carts and wagons may be adapted. The most accessible is a child's sled such as a Flexible Flyer. Sleds operate best on packed snow or rough ice. Most sleds have no brake so require careful handling to protect the dog.
5. *Toboggan*—A shaftless apparatus like the sled, unless it is an adapted version. The toboggan, like the sled, works best on well-packed snow or rough ice, but can also function on more loosely packed snow as it doesn't rely on runners.

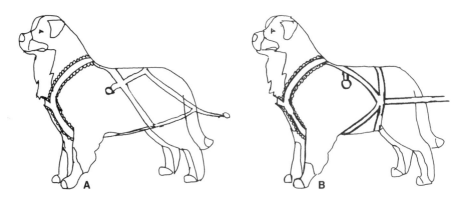

Two types of Siwash harness

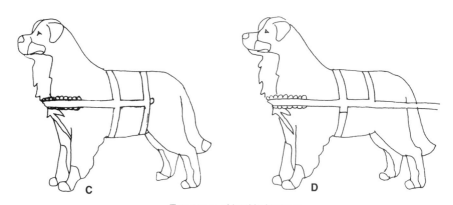

Two types of buckle harness

While the toboggan has more drag than the sled, when loaded properly it has ample capacity.

Types of Harness

There are two basic types of harness for carting.

1. *Siwash*—characterized by a properly fitted but flexible shoulder-neck collar. The dog pushes into this collar and the push is distributed evenly by the straps along the dog's sides. This harness allows complete freedom of movement of the dog's shoulder assembly and is therefore the safest form of harness to use for carting. (See Figures A and B, Two types of Siwash harness.)

190

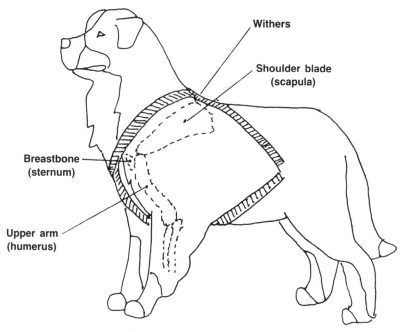

Withers

Shoulder blade
(scapula)

Breastbone
(sternum)

Upper arm
(humerus)

A properly fitted Siwash harness

2. *Buckle Harness*—This consists of one or more belly bands buckled around the dog's rig cage holding a cross-chest band in place. When pulling, the dog pushes directly into the cross-chest band. This type of harness hampers the movement of the shoulder assembly, and to be truly effective must rest directly on the sternum at all times. This type of harness often slides upward, causing the full weight of the load to rest on the dog's throat. Although readily available, these harnesses are not recommended for safe draft work. (See Figures C and D, Two types of buckle harness.)

The collar straps of a properly fitted Siwash harness should converge at the dog's breastbone with the upper portion of the harness snug at the base of the neck, the straps crossing at the withers. The pull is equal on both the lower and upper portions of the collar, keeping the collar properly positioned and the movement of the dog's shoulder assembly unrestricted. (See Figure E, A properly fitted Siwash harness.)

THE BERNESE MOUNTAIN DOG WORKING DOG CERTIFICATE

The idea of a Bernese Mountain Dog Club of America Working Dog Certificate was first proposed in 1979. Beverly Barney formulated standards for it closely following the Newfoundland Club of America WDC. This effort disappeared into the history books and was resurrected in 1984 when Beverly Barney was asked to simplify the wording. This too died of its own weight.

In October 1989 the enterprising members of the Bernese Mountain Dog Club of Nashoba Valley (New England) decided to test the feasibility and practicality of the original 1979 regulations proposed to the BMDCA.

They held the first formal Bernese Mountain Dog draft trial in the United States at Rocky Woods Reservation in Medfield, Massachusetts. The judges were Irene Feeley and Cindi Olson. Three teams were entered, one for "exhibition only," leaving two competitors: Debbie Mulvey with Berndach Erik v. Grundberg; Alison Jaskiewicz with Ch. Olympian's Oracle of Delphi, CD, TD; Adele Miller with Ch. Berndach Bridget, CD.

BMDCA DRAFT TITLES

Novice Draft Dog

Name (sex/date earned)	Owner/Breeder
Can. Ch. Bigpaws Banfield (D 5/92)	Bonnie Dick/Susan Quinn
Bluesky Matt Dillon v. Summit, CDX (D 9/91)	Kathy Heun & Kathy Roth/Kathy Roth
Elsa Undertow of Mt. Lore, CD (B 9/92)	Marjorie Cottle/Jean Bridge
Lisakarn America Bound Jerry (D 9/91)	Sara Dombroski, Alison Jaskiewicz, Deborah Mulvey/ Gordon Bridges
Lupine's Little Tugboat, CD (D 9/91)	Christopher & Marjorie Cottle/ Susan Muick & Joseph Giangarra

Name (sex/date earned)	Owner/Breeder
Ch. Nordstaaten's Emma, CDX (B 9/91)	Ruth Ballmer/Beverly Barney
Olympians Helen of Troy, CD (B 9/91)	Lisa Allen/Eileen Brouck
Ch. Olympians Oracle of Delphi, Am. Can. CD, TD (B 9/92)	Alison Jaskiewicz & Eileen Brouck/Eileen Brouck
Ch. Pinnacle's Andes v. Juster, CD (B 5/92)	Eden Jonas/Eden Jonas
Ch. Rosewood Benjamin Von Kayper, CDX (D 5/92)	Kay Morrow & Nancy Stewart/ Kay Morrow
Ch. Sandusky's Promises Promises, CD (B 9/91)	Elizabeth Zipsie & Sandra Ongemach/Sandra Ongemach
Schwartzeritter v. Mooseberry, CD (D 9/92)	Megan Huber/Kathy Jane Elders
Sennenhof Ilaria, CD (B 9/92)	Beverly Barney/Eve Menegoz
Ch. Shersan's Must Be Magic, CD (B 9/92)	Susan Sanvido & Carolyn Kinley/ Carolyn Kinley & Pat Dreisbach
Ch. Sojourner Shambhala, CDX (B 5/92)	Eden Jonas & Chuck Armatys/ Cheryl Campbell
Sudan Neuchatel v. Halidom, CD (B 9/91)	Susan & David Sanvido/Millicent & George Parliman
Ch. Travois Apollo v. Mystic Mtn., CD (D 5/93)	Lucy Vondracek & Karen Baru/ Diane Webber
Aiko Von Bernerliebe, CDX (D 5/92)	Fay & Doug Benson/Dwayne Byerly & Christina Ohlsen
Ch. Travois Apollo v. Mystic Mtn., CD (D 5/93)	Vondracek & Baru/Webber
Ch. Alpine Joy Deerpk Sgt. Harpo (D 9/93)	Mann/Aken
Blackguard Emma v. Bev's (B 9/93)	Bell/Burney
Brighteye Sizzlin Dragonfire (B 9/93)	Wetzel & Hotze/Hotze
Heidi-Ho Theodore Sage Bar (D 9/93)	Temples & Ramesdell/Chismar

Novice Draft Dog (*cont.*)

Name (*sex/date earned*)	Owner/Breeder
Ch. Konig Butcher Von Panache, CD (D 9/93)	Horney/Taylor & Ohlsen
Lake Haus Bravissimo Keji, CD (D 9/93)	Steele/Evert
Ch. La Plata Mountain's Big Deal, CDX (D 9/93)	Baru/Barr
Maitland's Mayor of Zurich (D 9/93)	Bertrand/McDonnell
Mr. Bosley (D 9/93)	Cottle/Wells
Roundtops Niedliche Baerin, CD (B 10/93)	Queer/Thomson
Berna Vombreiterweg II (B 10/93)	Wright/Heokstra & Perez
Dalleybeck's Jewel of Cresta, CD (B 10/93)	Kreutzfield/Reho

Draft Dog

Name (*sex/date earned*)	Owner/Breeder
Lisakarn America Bound Jerry, NDD, Can. CD (D 9/92)	Sara Dombroski, Alison Jaskiewicz, Deborah Mulvey/ Gordon Bridges
Olympians Helen of Troy, CD, NDD (B 9/92)	Lisa Allen/Eileen Brouck
Ch. Sojourner Shambhala, CDX, NDD (B 5/93)	Eden Jonas & Chuck Armatys/ Cheryl Campbell
Elsa Undertow of Mt. Lore, CD, NDD (B 9/93)	Cottle/Bridge
Sennenhof Ilaria, CDX, NDD (B 9/93)	Barney/Menegoz
Ch. Travois Apollo v. Mystic Mtn., CD, NDD (D 9/93)	Vondracek & Baru/Webber

Adele Miller, her Ch. Grunberg Iridescent Fire and a delighted passenger pose for the camera before the wagon starts to roll.

This antique goat wagon served as a picturesque, historical prop during the production of the AKC Bernese Mountain Dog breed Standard video in 1992.

Ch. Dallyback's First King George, owned by Nancy Fusilier, DVM, looking very grand in his dress antlers, is being assisted by daughter Katie and a Cocker Spaniel buddy on a "gift" run.

Each team received a certificate of participation from the Nashoba Valley Club and Ch. Olympian's Oracle of Delphi, CD, TD received a Certificate of Qualification.

The Nashoba Valley Club has continued its work in promoting carting. The first history-making event has become an annual activity in September in New England.

The following is the Draft Trial Certificate Proposal used at the 1989 trial.

Bernese Mountain Dog Draft Work Trial

Qualification A dog must pass each exercise in the draft trial to the satisfaction of the judge. A dog must pass all exercises at one trial to earn a certificate from the Bernese Mountain Dog Club of America.

Purpose The drafting exercises are designed to develop and demonstrate the inbred abilities of purebred Bernese Mountain Dogs in a land work capacity involving hauling. The Bernese Mountain Dog has historically functioned as a draft dog in various capacities, and performance of these exercises is intended to demonstrate skills resulting from both natural ability and training that are applicable to realistic work situations. Efficiency in accomplishment of tasks is essential; it is also desirable that the dog evidence willingness and enjoyment of the work in a combination of controlled teamwork with the handler and natural independence.

Objectives The drafting exercises are intended to allow Bernese Mountain Dog owners and their dogs to demonstrate draft work abilities. Since Bernese Mountain Dogs live in a variety of climates and perform draft work in a variety of situations, any of the following draft rigs may be used in performance of the exercises: cart, sled, toboggan, travois. The same rig must be used in all of the exercises.

Bernese Mountain Dog Draft Trial

EXERCISES (all completed off lead)

> 1. *Basic control*: heels at normal, fast and slow pace; turns; performs Down-Stay and Recall.

2. *Harness and hitch*: shows willingness to be harnessed and hitched to draft rig without shying.
3. *Control with distraction*: shows control in the presence of intriguing distractions while attached to draft rig.
4. *Basic command*: hauls forward, slows down, stops, backs up, stays two minutes, handler out of sight.
5. *Maneuvering*: negotiates circles, 90-degree turns, broad curves, narrow areas, removable obstacle.
6. *Distance freight haul*: half-mile; handler loads appropriate freight load range for dog and traverses a cross-country course with dog hauling loaded rig.

Regulations To qualify, the dog and handler will perform each of the following exercises:

1. *Basic control.* Dog is expected to perform this exercise as specified in the AKC *Obedience Regulations* for Heel Free, Long Down, and Recall. The Recall requires a proper finish. Dogs must perform on the first command.
2. *Harness and hitch.* Dog and handler enter ring; handler places dog on stay. Handler leaves dog, goes to ring entrance, gets harness and returns to dog. Dog stands on command for harnessing. Handler harnesses dog. Dog heels with handler to draft rig and stands to be hitched. When hitched, dog and handler move into position, indicating dog is ready to work.
3. *Control with distraction.* Dog performs both parts of exercise with empty draft rig.
   A. Dog moves (hauling) in a simple Heel next to handler. Another dog on leash with handler passes in front of hauling dog in motion. Distracter must cross within approximately ten feet of dog and keep moving in a straight path until well clear of team being tested.
   B. Dog moves (hauling) in a simple Heel next to handler. Distracter carrying a metal pie pan and metal spoon approaches team from front and bangs on pan with spoon at least once when approximately ten feet from team. Passing to rear of team, distracter bangs pan at least once when approximately ten feet from team. Pan must be banged five times.

4. *Basic command.* Dog performs exercises A through D while hitched to empty draft rig. Each exercise is performed on command and/or signal once, handler standing in front of dog.
   A. Haul forward.
   B. Slow down.
   C. Stop.
   D. Stay (two minutes), handler out of sight. Dog may be left standing, sitting or lying down, and must remain in that position until handler returns.
   E. Back up four feet.
5. *Maneuvering.* Performed with empty draft rig. Course includes:
   A. Circles (left and right).
   B. 90-degree turns.
   C. Broad curve.
   D. Movement through narrow area twelve inches wider than widest dimension of draft rig.
   E. Removable obstacle. Dog waits while handler removes obstacle, such as gate or tree branch. Dog and rig proceed through obstacle. Exercises D and E may be combined.
6. *Distance freight haul.* Handler loads draft rig with load appropriate to size and strength of dog, considering type of draft rig used. A simple half-mile, nonobstacle distance course is traversed. Judge must accompany handler and has authority to stop exercise if load is too great for dog in working conditions.

All exercises are performed off lead. Handlers may repeat commands and/or signals and/or praise, except during exercises 1 and 4 A, B, C, D. Except in harnessing and hitching, handler may not touch dog. Exercise 4E must be performed while dog is hitched if a wheeled vehicle is used. If a sled, toboggan or travois is used, dog performs exercise before being hitched, backing into hitching position. Cross-country exercise must be performed outside. All other exercises may be performed inside or outside, but not both. Praise between exercises is permitted.

The three participants in the first Bernese Mountain Dog drafting trial, their dogs and their wagons. They are (from left) Debora Mulvey with Berndach Erik v. Grunberg hitched to a sulky-style cart, Adele Miller with Ch. Berndach Bridgit, CD, hitched to a home-made box cart and Alison Jaskiewicz with Ch. Olympian's Oracle of Delphi, CD, TD, hitched to a child's converted wooden wagon. *Tom Jaskiewicz*

Gruezi Etain, Am., Can. CDX, TD, poses in the traces of a sulky-style cart.

199

Scoring

1. Basic control	pass/fail	0–5
2. Harness/hitch	pass/fail	0–5
3. Control with distraction	pass/fail	0–5
4. Basic command	pass/fail	0–5
5. Maneuvering	pass/fail	0–5
6. Distance freight haul	pass/fail	0–5

Dogs are scored on willingness, ability, enthusiasm, naturalness as a team and smoothness of performance. Dogs may earn 1 to 5 extra points in each exercise, depending on how they display these qualities. A total perfect score could be 30 points, allowing dogs that perform the exercises to qualify and receive extra credit for a smooth performance of a well-trained, eager worker.

These points are honor points, and any dog earning 20 or more points receives a With Honor certificate. A dog may enter additional trails after receiving a title in order to compete for a With Honor certificate.

To qualify, a dog must pass all exercises at one trial. The Bernese Mountain Dog Club of America provides a certificate for dogs that earn passing scores at drafting trials. A dog that passes is awarded a DD title. The title follows the dog's name and all AKC and CKC working titles. The American Kennel Club and the Canadian Kennel Club do not recognize the DD title. The letter H will appear in the title of any dog that passes a drafting trial with 20 or more honor points (i.e., DD/H).

The appropriate weight load is between 25 and 35 percent of the dog's weight (veterinarian certified) registered on a spring scale. Part or all of the weight derives from the weight and drag of the rig. On the same terrain as the cross-country course, a spring scale is attached to the rig at the same point where the harness is attached. Then the rig is moved by pulling on the spring scale. When the rig is moving, the spring scale is read. Weight must be added to the rig until the spring scale registers the correct poundage.

These regulations are constantly being updated. Contact the BMDCA for an updated edition of the *Draft Test Regulations* before entering a draft test.

DRAFT EQUIPMENT SOURCE GUIDE

Carts

Ikon Outfitters Ltd. (child's wagon conversion kits)
7597 Latham Road
Lodi, WI 53555

John DeGreef (sulky with wheels and runners)
Box 128
Bridgenorth, Ontario KOL 1HO
Canada

The Digas Company (sled conversions for cart)
10278 White Road
Linden, MI 48451

F. M. Lockhart (sulky)
1936 Dennis Lane
Santa Rosa, CA 95401

K-9 Sulkys
2406 North Wood Court
Claremont, CA 91711

Von Russ Giants
Harry Russ
123 Yeager Avenue
Forty Fort, PA 18704

Wagons

Lynchburg Hardware and General Store
Lynchburg, TN 37352

Tundra Outfitters
16438 96th Avenue
Nunica, MI 49448

Horse and Pony Wagons
14107 CR 42
Millersburg, IN 46543

Harness

Ikon Outfitters Ltd.
7597 Latham Road
Lodi, WI 53555

Nordkyn Outfitters
P.O. Box 3104
Federal Way, WA 98063

Patterns for Making Carts, Wagons and Travois

The Draft Equipment Guide (NCA Working Dog
    Committee)
Roger A. Powell
NCA Land Work Secretary
5208 Olive Road
Raleigh, North Carolina 27606

8

I Want to Be a Breeder!

PEOPLE DECIDE to become dog breeders for many reasons—they may feel their breed needs structural improvement and they believe they have the knowledge to accomplish this. Perhaps they feel their dogs have qualities that should be preserved by careful selective breeding that only they will accomplish. Many reasons are commendable—one, to make money, is not!

A reputable Bernese breeder finishes champions to establish breeding credentials, X-rays, checks eyes and spends a great deal of money on a wide variety of relevant priorities before breeding. Then there are stud fees, dewclaw removal, veterinary attention and lots of food before pups are sold. There may be replacement puppies—buying puppies back that don't work out as well as other unforseen mishaps. And if after all that there's any profit, it's probable that somebody added wrong or didn't count all the hours of personal time and labor. So if you're looking for a female for breeding to add to your income, remember the many unwanted pets sitting in shelters already. There are better paths to extra income.

But, if you are interested in improving the Bernese—begin

Ch. Arthos October v. Berndach (Aldo v. Kleinholz ex Ch. Grunberg Iridescent Fire), owned by Sharon C. Smith and bred by Adele Miller and Richard Volpe. Shown here with his owner, this dog was a top producer with twenty-three champion get and a noteworthy winner in his own right. *John L. Ashbey*

with a plan. Make certain your dog is temperamentally sound. Remember that breeding your cute bitch who only bites the mailman to a handsome stud who only growls at his owner may produce eight adorable pups who bite everyone—and you wouldn't want to get phone calls from the new owners (or their lawyers) who are being sued.

EVALUATION AGAINST THE STANDARD

The next step is to evaluate your bitch against the Bernese Mountain Dog Standard and decide what you want to improve structurally, what faults you want to correct while maintaining your bitch's good qualities. Example: If your bitch is lacking topline (has a dip), look to her parents. Are they lacking topline? If her sire has a great topline and her dam has one like hers, look for a stud with a strong topline who is not related to the dam of your bitch, but who could be related to the sire if the sire has no other faults you don't mind reproducing. (All dogs have faults, there are NO perfect dogs.) Breed to improve the topline while maintaining the good qualities. And remember, Rome was not built in a day—some faults can be corrected in one generation and some take a little longer or a lot longer. I find problems with shoulder angulation and layback one of the hardest to correct and one of the easiest to loose. Pick the puppy with the best of your original qualities plus the improvement you bred for.

HIPS, ELBOWS AND EYES

Even the most temperamentally sound and beautiful dogs should be evaluated for genetic faults such as hip and elbow dysplasia and eye problems. There are two recognized organizations that evaluate hips.
1. OFA—Orthopedic Foundation for Animals, Inc.
2. GDC—Institute for Genetic Disease Control in Animals
They are alike in that they both require radiographs (X-rays) well positioned with good film contrast. This is important, so ask around for a vet skilled in this procedure. The radiograph must have perma-

Ch. Trilogy's Title Role (Ch. Broken Oaks Dieter v. Arjana ex Ch. Texas Tiffany Vombreiterweg, CDX), owned and bred by Susan Tramp, is the dam of seventeen champions.

nent dog identification in the film emulsion, so take a copy of your dog's AKC registration certificate with you. You will also be asked to complete and sign the application form and enclose the proper fee.

The two registries are different in that OFA will not issue a number and declare the dog free of canine hip dysplasia (CHD) or elbow dysplasia until the age of twenty-four months. GDC will issue a number at twelve months. OFA does not disclose information about dogs that are dysplastic; only those that receive numbers are of public record. At OFA the fee is the same to have a dog's hips evaluated by its veterinarians whether it receives a number or not. GDC returns your submission fee if your dog is found to have congenital hip or elbow dysplasia and it is of public record that your dog is or is not affected. GDC also encourages entire litters to be evaluated, as they recommend breeding from dogs that show

206

Ch. Camelot's Hello Dolly (Ch. Jocky de Vilmoulin ex Ch. Starcrest Carri On v. Attlee), owned by Art and Gwen Russel, is the dam of ten champions.

William Gilbert

the largest number of normal progeny. I personally use both registries and find that they evaluate X-rays in the same manner, although I do prefer an open registry (open to the public, pass or fail).

There is also a recognized foundation for eyes—Certified Eye Registry Foundation—that will issue a certificate of clearance based on an evaluation by one of its board-certified ophthalmologists. The name is usually shortened to CERF.

To date, there are two known functional abnormalities of the eyelids or eyelashes that plague Bernese Mountain Dogs—entropion and ectropion. Both are visible to the trained eye. A symptom of entropion is eye watering in an eyelash pattern. Entropion is caused by the eyelashes turning in on the eye. This deformity can cause irritation to the cornea, considerable pain and a loss of sight if left uncorrected. Surgery is the only solution.

Ectropion is also a deformity that, although not as debilitating, is unsightly and does allow seeds and dust to enter the eye quite easily. This is a "pout" or "V" of the lower eyelid. This should not be confused with a minor loose eye that is not an actual eversion of the eyelid. There have also been a few recent and past cases of PRA (Progressional Retina Atrophy) and cataracts reported in Bernese. For a layperson to be sure his or her dog is free of these hereditary eye defects, an examination by a CERF board-certified ophthalmologist is the best method of detection.

PICKING A STUD DOG—AND A STUD DOG OWNER

When you have decided what you are looking for in a stud dog, begin by attending dog shows in your area and try to find a suitable dog among those in competition. If not, go through year-books available from the Bernese Mountain Dog Club of America for a suitable stud. You may also find a dog that has already finished his championship and is not currently being shown. Determine if this dog has been bred to any females similar to your own and see what he is producing. Many beautiful dogs do not reproduce themselves while many others do. Make sure you want puppies that could look more like him than your bitch.

When you have narrowed your choice to a few dogs, call and interview the owners. Are they experienced? Do you trust them? Your bitch may have to live with them for a short time. Ask them to evaluate their dog's faults and strong points. Ask them what qualities they think he is passing on, both physically and tempera-mentally. If this is the first time your bitch will be bred, ask if they will be able to perform an artificial insemination if necessary. Do they have enough space to accommodate your bitch, and will their dog be available at the time your bitch is due in season? This should all be finalized at least a month or more before your bitch is due to come in season just in case she comes in early. A backup dog is a good idea in the event something goes awry with your original plan.

Once the stud dog is chosen, start taking care of the details on your end. Make sure your bitch is in excellent health, is in good weight, is up to date on all her vaccinations and is clean and free

Ch. Kuster's Jocko of J-Bar (Ch. Clara's Christopher ex Alpstein Knight Bell), owned by Gretchen Johnson and Barbara Kuster. Shown here at five years of age, he is the sire of twenty-five champions.

of parasites. A litter will pull her down both in weight and overall condition. If she's healthy going into a litter it will be much easier to get her back into condition afterward. Of course there isn't much you can do about her coat—the majority of bitches will blow all coat three months after the birth of the litter. A coat supplement will help with the new coat.

Bred Jan	Due Mar	Bred Feb	Due Apr	Bred Mar	Due May	Bred Apr	Due Jun	Bred May	Due Jul	Bred Jun	Due Aug	Bred Jul	Due Sep	Bred Aug	Due Oct	Bred Sep	Due Nov	Bred Oct	Due Dec	Bred Nov	Due Jan	Bred Dec	Due Feb
1	5	1	5	1	3	1	3	1	3	1	3	1	2	1	3	1	3	1	3	1	3	1	2
2	6	2	6	2	4	2	4	2	4	2	4	2	3	2	4	2	4	2	4	2	4	2	3
3	7	3	7	3	5	3	5	3	5	3	5	3	4	3	5	3	5	3	5	3	5	3	4
4	8	4	8	4	6	4	6	4	6	4	6	4	5	4	6	4	6	4	6	4	6	4	5
5	9	5	9	5	7	5	7	5	7	5	7	5	6	5	7	5	7	5	7	5	7	5	6
6	10	6	10	6	8	6	8	6	8	6	8	6	7	6	8	6	8	6	8	6	8	6	7
7	11	7	11	7	9	7	9	7	9	7	9	7	8	7	9	7	9	7	9	7	9	7	8
8	12	8	12	8	10	8	10	8	10	8	10	8	9	8	10	8	10	8	10	8	10	8	9
9	13	9	13	9	11	9	11	9	11	9	11	9	10	9	11	9	11	9	11	9	11	9	10
10	14	10	14	10	12	10	12	10	12	10	12	10	11	10	12	10	12	10	12	10	12	10	11
11	15	11	15	11	13	11	13	11	13	11	13	11	12	11	13	11	13	11	13	11	13	11	12
12	16	12	16	12	14	12	14	12	14	12	14	12	13	12	14	12	14	12	14	12	14	12	13
13	17	13	17	13	15	13	15	13	15	13	15	13	14	13	15	13	15	13	15	13	15	13	14
14	18	14	18	14	16	14	16	14	16	14	16	14	15	14	16	14	16	14	16	14	16	14	15
15	19	15	19	15	17	15	17	15	17	15	17	15	16	15	17	15	17	15	17	15	17	15	16
16	20	16	20	16	18	16	18	16	18	16	18	16	17	16	18	16	18	16	18	16	18	16	17
17	21	17	21	17	19	17	19	17	19	17	19	17	18	17	19	17	19	17	19	17	19	17	18
18	22	18	22	18	20	18	20	18	20	18	20	18	19	18	20	18	20	18	20	18	20	18	19
19	23	19	23	19	21	19	21	19	21	19	21	19	20	19	21	19	21	19	21	19	21	19	20
20	24	20	24	20	22	20	22	20	22	20	22	20	21	20	22	20	22	20	22	20	22	20	21
21	25	21	25	21	23	21	23	21	23	21	23	21	22	21	23	21	23	21	23	21	23	21	22
22	26	22	26	22	24	22	24	22	24	22	24	22	23	22	24	22	24	22	24	22	24	22	23
23	27	23	27	23	25	23	25	23	25	23	25	23	24	23	25	23	25	23	25	23	25	23	24
24	28	24	28	24	26	24	26	24	26	24	26	24	25	24	26	24	26	24	26	24	26	24	25
25	29	25	29	25	27	25	27	25	27	25	27	25	26	25	27	25	27	25	27	25	27	25	26
26	30	26	30	26	28	26	28	26	28	26	28	26	27	26	28	26	28	26	28	26	28	26	27
27	31			27	29	27	29	27	29	27	29	27	28	27	29	27	29	27	29	27	29	27	28
				28	30	28	30	28	30	28	30	28	29	28	30	28	30	28	30	28	30		
				29	31			29	31	29	31	29	30	29	31			29	31	29	31		

Corresponding date calendar for breeding and whelping.

Since most responsible stud owners require a brucellosis test and a vaginal culture, it is a good idea to schedule these procedures a couple of weeks before your female is due in season. Be sure to ask the stud dog owner for a contract and list of dates on which your female was bred.

It's a good idea to keep a calendar, recording the number of days from the day she first came in season to the breeding days. In case the breeding doesn't take, you can refer back to this at the next season and perhaps do progesterone testing or vaginal smears to try to pinpoint her most fertile time.

One of my bitches consistently began breeding from her tenth day and always had seven pups in each litter. On one of her breedings, we had a narrow window of time and decided to do progesterone testing on her so we would spend the least amount of time between pickup and delivery. To our surprise she did not ovulate until her fifteenth day in season. This breeding produced nine puppies from artificial insemination. A little testing can really pay off in time saved both for you and the stud dog owner.

STUD FEES AND CONTRACTS

Each stud dog owner has his or her own method of doing business—but a few of the more common practices are:

1. Standard Contract—The stud dog owner receives a fee at the time of mating (usually based on the price of a show-quality puppy in the local area). They do not guarantee a live litter, only the mating. There is usually an offer of return service to the same bitch with the same dog if the mating isn't successful. This contract may also give the stud dog owner the right to use only his kennel name on stud fee puppies.
2. Flexible Contract—The stud owner takes an expense fee at the time of mating and the remainder of the fee when the puppies are born and the litter registration is signed. There is a guarantee of a minimum number of puppies to constitute a litter (usually three: one for the fee, one for the breeder, one for expenses). If the mating doesn't take, the stud dog owner may offer a return service to the same or another bitch you own, from the same stud you used or another from the same owner.
3. Swiss Contract—This type of breeding contract is an arrangement for paying the stud owner a set fee at the time of breeding, usually a nominal $100 to $200, and a fee "per puppy" after the litter is whelped, perhaps $100 a pup. This could be an asset when a small litter is involved, although a cap in the event of an unusually large litter is prudent.

Ask as many questions up front as possible. The more you nail down in writing, the better.

SHE'S PREGNANT! WHELPING A LITTER

Where your litter will be reared is of paramount importance. If you do not have a room that you can dedicate to delivering and raising a litter of Bernese, don't even consider breeding. Even the most fastidious bitch will break her housetraining after giving birth. It can't be helped, so plan on it—or take steps to protect your flooring.

Whelping a litter is exhausting, so make sure you are well rested days in advance as you may have to be up around the clock. I remember one bitch who began whelping at 11:05 P.M. on February 12 and continued until her last pup was born at 3:00 P.M. on February 13. All pups were healthy and vigorous. She just took her time.

Whelping Equipment and Supplies
(Arrange one week or more before due date.)

1. Whelping box
2. Mattress made out of foam covered with vinyl
3. Fitted double-bed sheets
4. Old clean towels, dried in the dryer to kill bacteria
5. Rubber gloves
6. Laundry basket
7. Cooler with removable lid
8. Heating pad covered with a towel
9. Clock to keep track of time between pups

As whelping time approaches, you'll be glad you requested a list of breeding dates from the stud dog owner—but now which one was it? Count sixty-three days (p. 210, Perpetual Whelping Calendar) from the first breeding and start taking her temperature well in advance of that date to establish her normal temperature. Her normal temperature may also vary slightly from morning to night. When you know what is normal for your bitch, you are ready for what will follow.

The first sign of impending labor is a temperature drop, usually from a normal of 101 degrees down to 99 degrees, or in that range. Some bitches only drop a degree or less. Then they begin nesting. This activity varies greatly from mild scratching to digging with such vigor that a hole in the floor seems sure to result. Usually by

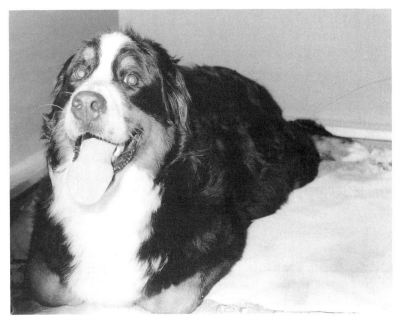

The onset of visible labor is marked by several signs. Two of the most reliable are heavy panting and dilated pupils as seen here.

As labor progresses the bitch is seen to push against her contractions as she holds her lowered head forward.

now, your sweet, adoring female has already excavated one or more holes in the yard large enough to conceal a sandbag. Since you won't let her whelp there, she will try to match the environment indoors. Try to convince her that the whelping box will do, and provide some bedding that she can tear up before she gets to the real thing. She will also want to go out to relieve herself every one or two hours. The onset of labor causes the feeling of a need to defecate and she may try to respond accordingly. This is normal, but as she begins to have contractions, stay with her. If she delivers a puppy outdoors, have a towel handy. You'll need it!

Actual laying-down, water-breaking, pushing labor will usually begin within twenty-four hours after the temperature drop, unless complications occur—and every time I think I have experienced them all, a new one comes along to keep me humble. There is not space in this book to cover all possibilities, so please consult the Bibliography for more reading on this subject.

Discuss in detail your upcoming litter with your veterinarian including contingency for a Caesarean section should your bitch need one. This is sometimes necessary to save either mom, the pups or both—and the eleventh hour is no time to look for a vet who is comfortable with this procedure in dogs.

As real labor begins, your bitch will begin to pant heavily, her eyes may dilate and she will begin little sessions of pushing in a sitting or laying position. If sitting, she will move her head out and forward and grunt a little with each push.

She will also turn and inspect her vulva every so often and lick or stare at the area. Check for vulva dilation. It will become very soft and enlarged as labor increases.

The next step is the breaking of the water. Your bitch will usually lick herself vigorously at this point and a pup will follow in about fifteen to thirty minutes. The puppy is usually born head-first, but not always. The mother will usually lick the sack off and start licking the puppy. If the afterbirth has been expelled with the pup, remove both and tear cords using a towel at both ends. This simulates the mother tearing the cord with her teeth, which crushes the blood vessels in the cord and reduces bleeding. As an alternative, use dull, sterilized scissors.

I don't often let the mother tear the cords herself as she sometimes tears them too close. I do let her consume a few of the

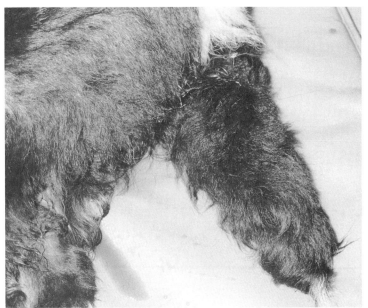

The "water bag" will appear immediately prior to the birth of the puppy and generally breaks during the birth process.

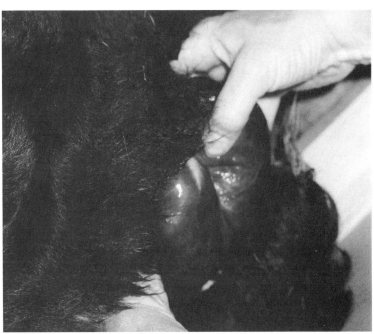

The first puppy emerges and the blaze on its head is clearly visible in this photo even though the amniotic sac is still intact.

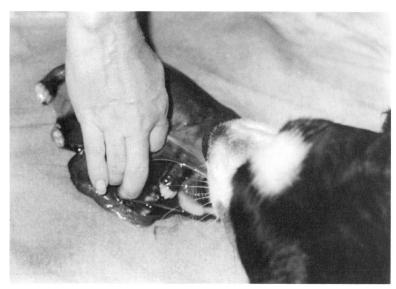

Unless the attendant chooses to do so, the mother dog will generally tear away the amniotic sac and wipe the birth fluids away from her newborn.

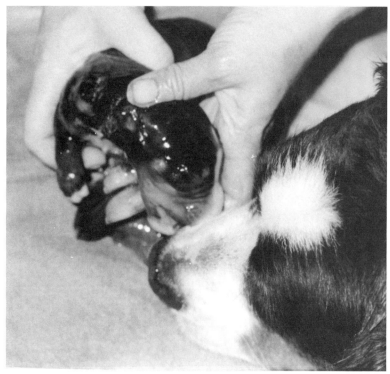

It is normal for the mother dog to sever the umbilical cord, and most breeders allow their bitches to do so. Vigilance is called for to prevent a bitch from biting the cord too short—a potentially dangerous possibility.

216

afterbirths. It seems to help stimulate labor, but eating too many causes diarrhea, so I keep the number down to a few.

Dry the pup thoroughly and rub it with a towel, then set the newborn aside in the cooler on a heating pad well wrapped in a towel so pups will not be burned. Keep the pad on a low-to-medium setting. If things slow down and the time lengthens between pups, allow the pups to nurse. This will also promote additional labor and the firstborn pups get a chance at some nutrition.

If labor slows down for longer than thirty minutes, take your new mom out for a walk. This will often get things going again, but take a towel in the event of a sudden birth, and don't go far.

Some pups are large and mom may need a hand. First, have her stand—if you can see the head or feet and they appear and disappear, get her to take a walk. This usually helps the puppy to reappear. Don your rubber gloves and grasp the pup gently but firmly, and pull downward working with the contractions. By the way, feet first, or breech birth, is also normal and is seen in about 40 percent of deliveries.

The bitch may take it from here and expel the pup and afterbirth. If not, you will have to sever the cord, remove the pup from the sack and wait until she forces out the placenta on her own. This will usually occur with the next onset of contractions.

A pup that is slow to be delivered because of its size will often be out of the sack and blue. Quick work can save the day. First clear the lungs of fluid by suction, then hold the puppy with its head lowered to allow gravity to assist. If the puppy is not breathing, lay the pup in your hands, head held securely between your fingers. Raise the puppy a full arm's length above your head and, holding it securely, sling it in a semicircular motion toward the floor. Keep the pup well supported and do this as many times as needed to clear the air passages. I have sometimes done this ten to twenty times to get a puppy breathing.

As soon as the puppy is breathing evenly, let it rest on the wrapped heating pad before nursing. Keep it warm, and as soon as its breathing comes normal, put it in with mom to nurse. She will also nudge and lick the puppy to get it moving. By this time the box should be getting pretty messy; just strip off your first sheet, throw it in your waiting laundry basket and put on a fresh sheet.

Between puppies I record time of birth, size, sex, markings

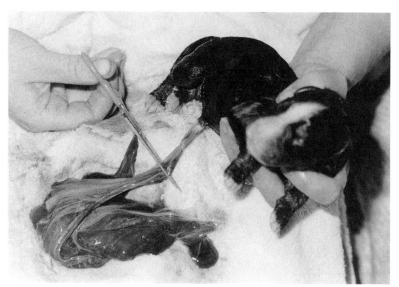

If the bitch requires assistance for any reason, the attendant should be ready to step in. If puppies are being born in rapid succession, it might be necessary to sever the cord on one puppy while the bitch is busy with another.

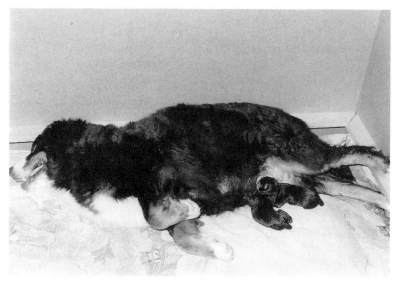

The nursing activity of the first arrivals usually will stimulate fresh birth contractions. Here the bitch is pushing against the sides of the box with her hindlegs, indicating that another puppy is soon to emerge.

218

Just born and not yet fully emerged, this puppy was born out of its sac with no ill effects. Such births are common but can involve risk to the puppy.

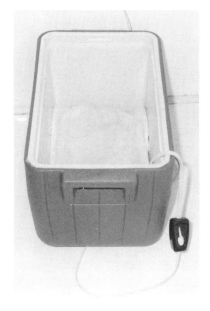

Everything needed for a whelping should be ready in advance. This cooler contains a heating pad in the *On* position and covered with a towel. It is an ideal place to deposit puppies during subsequent deliveries as well as a temporary incubator for traumatized newborns.

The new family safely delivered, clean and contented.

and whether they were born with rear dewclaws or not. I check bites—if they are undershot, overshot, scissors or level now, they will be later.

As soon as all puppies have arrived, clean the box, using another fresh sheet. By now the dam will need her rear rinsed in the tub and dried. Then return the happy family to its clean surround-

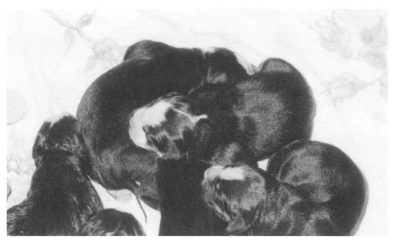

White head markings appear very large at birth and gradually recede as the puppy grows.

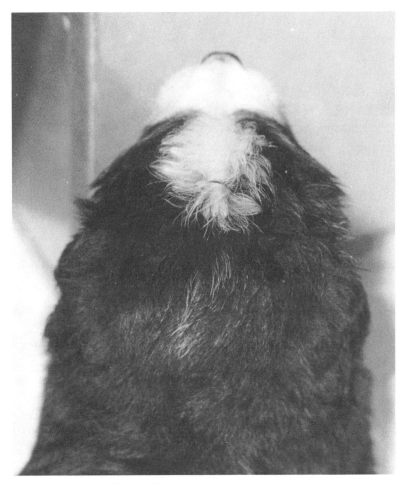

By five weeks the white markings on the puppy in the previous photo are greatly reduced and may become even smaller by maturity.

ings and take a nap yourself—with one ear open to the puppy room. Your bitch will be very tired and could easily roll over on a pup.

The next day, take a good look at markings. My first Bernese litter included a number of pups with white streaks running down the backs of their heads and white spots on the backs of the necks. I was convinced they were all horrible mismarks and that there wouldn't be a show pup in the bunch. A few weeks later at a match I related this to three other Berner folks who all came over to see the litter and proclaimed in unison, ''Oh, that will fade!'' I was very skeptical, but sure enough, by the time they were eight weeks old the white streaks and spots were no longer visible. Three champions resulted from that litter. Check what you think may be a mismark carefully. If there is no pink skin under the white hair, only blue, the white will most likely fade.

What about the rust or tan markings? At birth, these are a muddy color, often with black penciling mixed in, especially in the dogs that mature to a deep rust. This too is temporary, so don't despair. Bernese are also often born with pink noses that turn black as the pigment develops.

STUD DOG MANAGEMENT

No discussion of breeding would be complete without a few words about stud dog management. If your first Bernese is a male, is successfully shown to his championship and is free of the hereditary defects we have discussed, someone may approach you about breeding him.

If so, you must first consider the health and well-being of your dog. Make sure the owners of the female have the bitch tested for brucellosis, that a vaginal culture is done and that any infections are treated before breeding takes place. A brucellosis test for your male is a good idea as well. A great many male Bernese have reduced sperm counts because of infections contracted from bitches during breeding. Infections of this type in males usually show no outward signs until after the damage is done.

Keep in mind that it is better to prove an inexperienced dog on an experienced bitch. If, however, your first avenue into breeding begins with two maiden animals, find an experienced breeder in your area and ask for help in handling the breeding. Getting a successful breeding is often much more difficult than it sounds. Also, alert the owners of the bitch and ask them to arrange to have a backup dog standing by—just in case.

Finally, you should be aware of an important point of breeding "etiquette." Many times an inexperienced owner proclaims, "I'm looking for a female to breed to my male," and he doesn't mean he wants to buy a puppy. This is considered bad manners. You can extoll the merits of your male in a variety of ways, but do not directly approach owners of bitches to promote your stud. Remember, they will have to pay you a stud fee or give you a puppy, as well as raise and sell the litter. They will be the ''breeders'' so the decision of which stud to use is theirs. They should approach you, and not vice versa.

The experience of raising a well-bred litter of Bernese puppies is equally educational, exciting and exasperating. For the serious breeder, nothing is more important than working with successive generations of quality animals.

9

Raising Bernese Puppies

BIRTH TO EIGHT WEEKS

The First Week

This is a critical time in the life of a puppy. During the neonatal period, puppies cannot maintain or regulate their own body heat. You may find it necessary to elevate the temperature in the whelping room to 75 degrees or thereabouts, although many Bernese seem to do quite well in a cool room. This may be a result of their background as rugged farm dogs. I do not recommend using heating pads in the whelping box as I have had puppies crawl under the pad and become suffocated. I have also had a bad experience with a heating lamp over the whelping box, which exploded when a bitch came inside from being out in a light snow and shook herself. The best way to determine the correct temperature is by observing the puppies. If they are too warm, puppies will spread out from one another, pant and try to expose their stomachs to as much air as possible. On the other hand, if puppies are too cold, they will huddle together and curl up in tight balls to warm their stomachs. In either case, they will often cry, although Bernese are quite stoic and may not make a fuss. Normal body temperature for pups during the first two weeks is 94 to 97 degrees. Healthy puppies are warm, quiet and seldom cry unless they are hungry. Normal pups also seem to constantly twitch or change position even while sleeping. They are warm to the touch when being handled and their skin feels healthy and filled out. Beware of the puppy that does not move around or flex his head to one side in search of a nipple and is cold to the touch. This pup could be seriously ill. Keep a close eye on him. A dam will often push away a cold puppy, so be sure to consult a veterinarian promptly, as puppies can fade rapidly. Normal puppy behaviors are 1) rooting: poking their noses against everything searching for food, 2) sucking: the reflex of sucking on everything resembling a nipple and 3) the righting reflex: automatically turning on their stomachs or sides when placed on their backs.

Your only duties during this period are observing the puppies' behavior, maintaining a comfortable temperature in the room and occasionally letting mom out to relieve herself. This is a delightful time. The puppies depend on stimulation from their dam to urinate or defecate during the first sixteen days, so the bedding remains clean except for the dam's discharge and foreign matter brought in from successive trips outside. Her licking is very important to the puppies at this time. Should she have undergone a Caesarean section, you may have to encourage her by applying a little butter to their bellies, to give her the idea. Instinct usually takes over at the point of need.

Weight gain is the surest way to determine if pups are thriving. They should gain weight daily and will have at least doubled their birth weight by seven to ten days.

A good way to keep track of this weight gain is a simple chart on each pup. Weigh them every two or three days for the first two weeks, then once weekly. Respiration and heart rate of newborn pups is much slower during the first couple of weeks; often pups that appear to have a problem are just fine. On the first day 8 to 18 breaths per minute and 120 to 150 heartbeats per minute are normal. These will accelerate to 15 to 35 breaths per minute and 180 to 220 heartbeats per minute by five weeks.

Learn to recognize these signs of a sick or fading puppy:
The puppy

- does not exhibit jerking, twitching sleep patterns.
- is cool to the touch, skin is limp.
- does not gain weight.
- will move away or be pushed away from littermates and dam.
- loses (or doesn't have) the rooting or sucking reflex.

Hopefully your puppies and their dam will be healthy and all you will have to do for the first few weeks is change the bedding.

When the pups are two or three days old they will require dewclaw removal. This is minor surgery and easily performed by your veterinarian, who should be alerted to one peculiarity of Bernese—double rear dewclaws. These bear mentioning as their appearance can be quite disturbing. My first impression of these double dewclaws was, "This puppy has six toes! Oh dear God, he's deformed." I had never seen this type of dewclaw before. It actually appears to be one or sometimes two additional toes, not just smaller useless appendages that are commonly considered dewclaws. They can give an almost "monkey paw" look to the back feet and are routinely removed with no ill effects. I usually take the dam along on this trip for a checkup and to make sure there are no signs of infection. Your trusty cooler will come in handy for this trip—just unplug and away you go. If it is winter, preheat the car, put the lid on the cooler and carry the litter to the car. Once in the car, remove the lid, but keep it handy to pop back on going from the car into the veterinarian's office.

A rather common condition in Bernese puppies is umbilical hernias. In other breeds these are less common and must usually be surgically reduced. Often they are considered a genetic fault that should be excluded from breeding programs. In Bernese Mountain Dogs hernias are a normal occurrence and rarely need surgery. Many veterinarians, my own included, jump to the conclusion at eight weeks that surgery will be unavoidable but at six months find it completely unnecessary.

Weeks Two and Three

Up until now you have been examining these new little whelps for markings, head shape and bodies. That's about all there was—every time you try to cuddle the little guys they root or thrash around looking for a nipple. They are blind and deaf and not a lot of fun. However, I firmly believe in handling puppies on a limited basis (by family members) even at this stage. Each member of our family holds a pup close to their skin for ten to fifteen minutes each evening while reading or watching TV.

Somewhere around ten days to two weeks little cracks begin to open in the corners of their eyes. Now you hold your breath—will any of them have blue eyes? Well, they just might. The blue eye inheritance pattern is very elusive. Even though both parents may have dark brown eyes, they can both carry the blue-eyed gene. If this were the case, 25 percent of the litter would show blue eyes and be pure for the trait, 25 percent would have brown eyes and they would be pure for the trait and 50 percent of the litter would have brown eyes, but would be carrying the gene for blue eyes. That is, if this were a nice clean pattern—of course it rarely is. Perhaps only one parent had a blue-eyed gene, then there could be

The trait for blue eyes exists within the gene pool of the Bernese Mountain Dog and is considered a disqualification in the Standard. Dogs exhibiting the trait should not be bred from, but can make lovely pets.

an entire litter of brown-eyed individuals with 50 percent of that litter carrying the blue-eyed gene. In another example, albeit an unacceptable one, a pure blue-eyed dog bred to a pure brown-eyed dog could come up with an entire litter of brown-eyed dogs that were all carrying the gene for blue eyes. So don't feel bad if you come up with a blue eye now and then. Breeding two dark-eyed parents does not ensure brown-eyed offspring. The trait is in the gene pool or it wouldn't be a disqualification. The blue-eyed pups also make wonderful pets, so find pet homes for those you breed and move on. Of course if you begin to produce a large number of blue eyes you should definitely evaluate your breeding program. A blue eye that will stay blue (all Bernese have dark blue eyes as babies) is the color of a china plate, a rather watery light blue. Some blue eyes have pie wedges of brown in them, as some brown eyes have wedges of blue.

The next exciting event in the life of a litter is the opening of the ears. This happens about three days after the eyes open. Now they cannot only see mom, they can hear her too! Up until now the most you have had to do was to move the pups to their heated cooler, let mom out and change the sheets (probably because of mom's discharge, as Bernese seem to discharge for up to four to five weeks after delivery). The other little chore that should be kept up is nail clipping (using human nail clippers). This might be needed as often as every other day. Clip off the sharp ends and if you happen to hit the quick, just apply a little coagulant powder to stop the bleeding.

With ears and eyes open and functional, puppies are ready for action. They will now begin to be noticeably wet. Changing the sheets now becomes a losing battle and it's time to add the papers. If there is a newspaper publisher in your area, call and ask if you can buy shredded end rolls in bales. These papers make raising puppies delightful. They have no ink and are shredded, giving them volume. The puppies must hop through the paper to get around and therefore develop lovely muscle tone. Shredded papers also keep moisture and feces away from the puppies, as the shreds ''heal'' over the soiled spots.

Now is also the time to begin a little supplemental feeding of the puppies. The dam has been on two to three times her usual ration along with 10 percent yogurt, egg yolk and raw liver alternated. In

Shredded white paper, as described in the text, is added to the whelping box when the puppies are about two weeks old. This bedding provides a warm, clean, absorbent environment in which Bernese puppies can spend a happy infancy.

our kennel, her usual ration is Natural Life Condition Food mixed half with Natural Life Lamaderm, 500 mg. vitamin C, 400 mg. vitamin E and 30–50 mg. zinc. To this we also add a little Solid Gold Concept-a-Bitch. The pups are started on Natural Life Puppy Food soaked in hot water to which is added a little low-fat cottage cheese, yogurt or skim milk powder. The food is soft but not watery. Care must be taken with fatty supplements in puppy food as it tends to cling to the puppies' tender noses. If mom is not fastidious about cleaning them, it can lead to puppy pyoderma, which must be treated with antibiotics to avoid scarring. At about two weeks many breeders also begin the first worming. I like to alternate between Nemex and Strongid-T every two weeks until eight weeks of age. Also, at this time you can begin to get a clearer picture of the markings, but keep in mind that it always seems as though the whole dog grows and the markings stay the same.

The early feedings can be quite successful with an old cake pan. The puppies seem to fall in the food, lick it off each other and just play around for the first few days. One to two feedings of this kind a day is all that is necessary until they get used to the idea.

Here is a graphic comparison of how head markings change. At three weeks this puppy's blaze is very wide, but by fourteen months the same dog shows a very thin blaze indeed.

Young puppies, left to their own devices, will frequently "wear" a portion of their meals. The food pan shown here, known as the "flying saucer," tends to keep youngsters clean during and after mealtimes.

As they begin the third week, puppies get much more serious about food. At this point some breeders switch puppies to a flying saucer dish. A wonderful invention, its unique design keeps the pups out of the dish (somewhat!).

This is also the period when nose and lip pigment begins to fill in, although this process can take from four to six months to complete. I find the clearer the white on the face the longer this process takes, although this can vary among families. The photo at the start of this chapter shows a fully pigmented litter at under six weeks of age. Other Bernese puppies can take much longer to acquire all pigment, but noses should be completely black by six months.

Weeks Four to Six

Now your work really begins. These are no longer quiet, sleepy babies, they are growing dogs, all eight or ten of them. At this point they want either you (the food person) or their mom (the milk wagon). I begin to slowly wean my puppies at around four weeks as they have now outgrown the whelping box and have been moved

Pigment takes time to fill in with the Bernese. The noses and lips of these two-week-old puppies show a considerable amount of pink.

By age eight weeks the puppy on the far left of the preceding photo has achieved a considerable amount of dark pigment. Eventually, any remaining areas of pink will be overspread by black.

At age four weeks these puppies have been moved to a roomy 5 × 10 foot pen.

Puppies at four weeks will have been started on solid food, but will still try to nurse from their mother when she comes to visit. At this age, bitches that will still allow nursing will usually do so in a standing position. Note that the bitch is also beginning to shed, a normal consequence of having a litter.

into a wire enclosure familiarly termed an exercise pen and further shortened to "X-pen." They also have developed incredible toenails and teeth. The dam will begin to stand while nursing so the pups can no longer knead her as they nurse. (Kneading is like kneading bread. The pups pump up and down against their mother with their front feet as they nurse.) At this point I begin to let mom in to nurse only in the morning while I'm making the puppies' breakfast, and again at night.

This large area shown in the accompanying photos makes it easier for mom to get in with the pups and gives them much more room for muscle development. I continue using the shredded papers and, weather permitting, the puppies are allowed an occasional jaunt outside.

When the puppies are between five to six weeks of age, I grade the litter. Gretchen Johnson, breeder of the first Best in Show Bernese, told me about this time period, and it has always been just right. I videotape the puppies set up on a grooming table. I measure the length of the shoulder blade and the length of the upper arm to find that the pup is equal in these measurements. Then I look for the angle that these two bones make. I next check shoulder width and layback. I'm looking for a shoulder no wider than an inch combined with a decent layback—they usually go together. Then I suspend the puppy with all fours off the ground to check topline. If the dog roaches or is swaybacked or dips behind the shoulders, it has no place in my breeding program. Next, I drop the front and rear. However it falls gives me the picture I need to see. A slight toeing out is normal, but an exaggeration will stay that way. A rear or a front that drops close should be avoided. This is also true for toeing in. The most important factor is the overall outline of the dog. Is it pleasing, does the neck slope smoothly into the back with a nice withers or does it join abruptly with a flat withers? What you see now, with a little variation, is what you get later.

At six weeks the puppies get their first health checks and vaccinations. I don't give my own shots as I want my veterinarian to check for heart murmurs and any medical problems that may not be obvious. The pups are now ready for some serious socialization. In good weather I set up a large exercise pen outdoors with a little obstacle course in it. This consists of some large plastic flower pots with the bottoms cut out for puppies to crawl through, some old

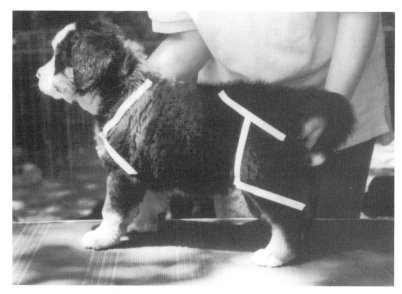

Measuring for front and rear angulation

Holding the puppy in this position allows the experienced breeder to accurately evaluate the topline.

This action is referred to as *dropping the front*. The puppy is actually lifted off its front legs and gently lowered, not dropped, into its natural position. Properly done, it will allow an accurate evaluation of the front assembly.

The corresponding action to evaluate a puppy's hindquarters is called *dropping the rear* and is performed by gently lowering the puppy by its tail and observing the position of the rear legs.

What you see is what you get. Would you want an adult dog with this outline in your breeding program?

plastic spools that wire is packed on and a few milk jugs washed out and with the caps removed. I gave up buying commercial toys long ago as the puppies prefer these homemade versions. Little walks around the yard and lots of carrying around are all the pups need to keep them busy and well socialized at this age.

Weeks Six to Eight

Clean, clean, clean describes this period the best. If you have been using the X-pen successfully until now, keep a watchful eye. A large litter may discover that if they all get together and jump in the same place they can knock the pen over. You may have to do a little anchoring. A bungee cord attached to the wall behind the pen will often do the trick. Water dishes are now replaced by water buckets clipped to the X-pen to prevent spilling the contents—a favorite puppy pastime. Some pups will crawl in the water in warm weather to cool off.

In the summer I sometimes switch to pine shavings for bedding when the puppies reach this age. The pine keeps the odor down and if you like to garden, the used shavings make great mulch for your flower beds.

Your puppies are rapidly approaching eight weeks, so it is time to get everything in order for the puppies' departure. For each puppy you sell, your puppy package should include:

1. A four to five generation pedigree showing as many OFA and GDC numbers as you can research out—at least both parents. Also include as many titles as possible, not just championships but top producers and number of get, obedience, tracking and carting titles, and whatever else is applicable.

2. A feeding schedule, and a small supply of the food the puppy has been eating to tide the new owner over until he or she can purchase a larger quantity of the same food.

3. Photos of both parents and any other related dogs whose photos are available. This was once impractical because of the cost, but with today's color copiers this is no longer a serious problem and makes a nice impression on new owners.

238

4. Instructional literature of your choice on all matters relating to management needs of a growing Bernese puppy.

Every buyer of a new Bernese Mountain Dog puppy should receive just such a package.

PUPPY SALES CONTRACTS

This is a sticky area for both the breeder and the buyer and both parties often have very good reasons for the limitations. I will first tell you the kind of sales agreement, or contract, I use and why, as I know this arrangement best. My agreement says I have first rights to buy the puppy back at the original purchase price should the buyer decide he or she doesn't want it, no questions asked. This evolved out of a desire for always knowing where our breeding was and not wanting any to ever end up in a shelter. The remainder of the contract discusses the terms for showing and breeding, and they are:

1. The dog's hips and elbows must be X-rayed at one or two years of age, and the findings must be submitted to either Genetic Disease Control to or Orthopedic Foundation for Animals to obtain a number.
2. The owner and breeder must agree, either by videotape study or personal examination, that this dog is of sufficient quality to reasonably complete the requirements for a championship.
3. Or, we may agree that even though this dog has some characteristic that may make it difficult to obtain a championship (scar from an injury, dislike of the show ring), he or she is still a desirable breeding animal.

Once these conditions are met, I either sign off the co-ownership or reverse the limited registration for the dollar difference between pet quality and show quality. With this contract the buyer does not pay for a show-quality dog until he or she has one.

Other types of contracts include what I call the chain letter contract. This contract operates much like a chain letter for the breeder. I was involved in one of these long ago in another breed and would never do this again.

This is a co-ownership with puppies back, such as first and third pick bitch, and the breeder usually has approval of the stud dog, often recommending his or her own stud, therefore receiving three pups instead of two. Now the chain begins, the breeder sells those three puppies on co-ownerships with two or three puppies back and, of course, only the original kennel name is used so they all appear to the casual observer to have been bred by the original kennel. The seller is now up to between six and nine pups back and hasn't even whelped a litter—and this is all from the one original dog sold. What about any others that may have been sold that year? Perhaps only five show bitches are sold on co-ownership and two are not X-rayed. From just three bitches the breeder will receive six to nine pups that will generate twelve to eighteen salable dogs that will generate another twenty-four to thirty-six salable puppies, ad infinitum. This contract often leaves the original buyer with the pets while the original breeder winds up with the cream of the litter. I doubt that any breeder has a dog you need badly enough to become a link in their chain. If you must have a dog out of this stock, look around for someone who has already signed off one of these pyramids and buy from them. Put the seller's kennel name on your new Berner—after all, he or she was listed as the breeder.

In a more equitable type of co-ownership a puppy is sold at pet price and the breeder retains co-ownership with the buyer until, in the case of a female, the buyer breeds her and gives one pup back to the breeder, who then signs off. If a male is involved the breeder may retain co-ownership but have no percentage of outside stud fees, only the right to breed his or her own bitches to this dog at no charge. In this type of agreement the breeder's kennel name is used in naming puppies. This contract simply allows a small breeder to retain rights to some valuable breeding stock that might otherwise be lost because of a limit on the number of dogs he or she can keep or because of other lifestyle constraints.

A co-ownership with every *other* litter going back to original breeder works well, with people who have the same values and live in close proximity. In this situation there is usually no charge for the pup or pet price if the breeder shares show expenses. Both parties share either the risk that the dog will not mature as hoped or the bounty if it does. When it's your litter, you pick the stud, make the arrangements and put your kennel name on the litter. The show dogs are yours to keep or sell as well as the pets. When it is the breeder's litter, he or she handles the mating, whelps the litter and in general shares in the work as well as the rewards. Usually the co-owner receives the first litter for having raised the dog, but if you are insecure about who to breed to and want the breeder's input, let him or her breed and whelp the first litter. This gives you the opportunity to see what that combination produces, find out if a Caesarean is involved or if whelping difficulties are encountered. If you co-own a male, hopefully the breeder will prove him on one of his or her own bitches. This will give you the opportunity to see how eager he is to breed, and you'll have the chance to learn how to handle him in a breeding situation.

There are probably many other types of arrangements. These, however, are the most familiar.

GOING HOME

Today's the day! You've done all the research, gone to see the kennel, sire and dam, met the breeder (or done it all in photos and long-distance calls) and now you are ready to pick up your puppy. Unless you are having the puppy shipped and picking it up at the airport, you should purchase a crate. You may be thinking, "I'll hold this new little baby on my lap!" Just remember you probably have a considerable drive, and without a crate, you'll be sorry. Sharp little puppy teeth get old very quickly and so does "Mommy, he's biting me," as you pass your new charge from lap to lap to reduce the complaining. Puppies will be puppies, so prepare for the worst and be grateful for any help you get, such as the puppy falling asleep as you drive.

What type of crate should you get? The definitive answer is a wire suitcase crate for car travel and household use. These crates are just what the name implies, a wire crate that folds up to suitcase size, complete with handles. They are extremely easy to work with and fold up instantly for easy handling. Buy a crate that is the correct size for your adult dog, along with a crate divider. This arrangement eliminates the need to buy new crates every three months as your puppy grows. Each time the puppy seems a little too crowded in the crate you simply move the divider to make it more spacious.

Puppyhood passes all too quickly, but as the Bernese grows it will become obvious to a loving family what a wonderful companion this beautiful breed can be.

It is also important to make an appointment with your veterinarian for the first possible day after you return home with the puppy. This is simply for a "well puppy" check. Most breeders insist on this so your vet confirms that your puppy is indeed in good health as promised by the breeder. This is also the time to bring the immunization and worming record your breeder has supplied so your vet can set up a schedule to complete your puppy's shots. On your next visit, it is advisable to take along a stool sample so your vet can check for parasites. Even with an every-two-week schedule of treatments, some worms may still survive.

If you do not have a regular veterinarian, shop around and choose one wisely. Ask the advice of other pet owners as well as breeders in your area. Gather all the facts and make your decision an informed one. Consider your sources—are they level-headed, fair and from the same economic level as yourself? You must be comfortable with your dog's doctor and only you are able to know if he or she inspires your total confidence.

Now you are really ready to go. But when you get there how will you know which one to pick? If you are purchasing a show prospect, go back to "Raising Puppies, Weeks Four to Six," and run through all those same tests. If the breeder does not have a grooming table, ask to put a towel on a kitchen table or counter. Take a video camera, tape the litter and ask to play the tape back on their TV set. You can certainly ask for the breeder's input. The breeder will have experience with similar genetic combinations and the look of the pups at this age. The breeder may also be able to show you videotapes or stills of earlier litters to help with your decision. Ultimately, you will find it most satisfying to pick the pup you think will be the show dog. In order to do this try to attend many shows before picking your puppy and get a sense of what you like and don't like. You may make a mistake the first time, but that's part of the learning experience, and if you continually rely on the breeder, how will you ever learn? On the other hand, if you are picking a pet, look for the one you bond with, if there is a choice available. In both cases you may have been assigned a pick and that is that. Some litters are presold in this manner. Check with the breeder well in advance of pickup day and ask the policy. If Mom and Dad were friendly and outgoing after being properly introduced, your new pup should be just fine. Bernese are still in rather short supply so a puppy may be hard to find. Most prospective owners get on a list with a particular breeder and wait. A sure way to be put at the bottom of any breeder's list is to call every breeder whose name you can find.

SETTLING IN

You finally arrive home with your new puppy! Puppy-proof your home in advance of the puppy coming in. Put away all important items that you cannot afford to lose, as puppies get into everything. One room should be the "puppy's room." The kitchen is one possibility, but not one with slippery floors on which the pup's feet constantly slide out from under him. This can lead to hip dysplasia in a pup with normal hips. We train puppies to stay in their room even with the door open. This breed is extremely easy to train if they think an action has merit, and for some reason this one clicks with them. We simply put them in their room and quietly leave (this works very well if they are asleep). When they wake up and begin to leave the room or just follow us out, we charge back toward them stamping our feet loudly and saying "Noooooo!" This loud, long "No" is reserved strictly for the dogs and is never used except in their correction. As soon as they cross the threshold into "their room" the correction voice stops and we immediately begin to praise them: "Good bunny, what a cutie, yeah, pupper-stuffer," etc. What you say is not as important as the tone of voice. It is a high, happy voice that contrasts with your low, corrective voice. Depending on how self-assured the pup is, this can take from two sessions to twelve, but it usually works quite quickly. We have had pups that learned this in one correction, but they were extremely well bonded to us.

The first night may be easy as the puppy may be exhausted from all the attention of the family and sleep through the night. But the worst is yet to come. At age eight weeks, I usually leave puppies loose in their room with some papers down and their crate door open. I don't believe in strict crate housebreaking until around age four months. If you don't mind getting up during the night, put your crate divider in and leave just enough room for the puppy to lie down. Put the pup in the crate with no bedding to absorb urine and go to bed. Whenever the puppy cries, get up and take him out to make sure he does something then go back to bed. You might have to put the pillow over your head so you won't hear the puppy complaining. After all, he's awake and ready to play—four hours of sleep is plenty for him. What's wrong with you anyway—you're not a lot of fun. If you decide to put the crate in the basement or somewhere else where the puppy will not be heard, you will be creating problems for you and the dog later on. Bernese are large dogs and take a long time to develop. If your pup is forced to hold back all night because you can't hear him cry to go out, you are asking for developmental problems such as kidney infections and bladder infections, and even stool eating to try hiding the mistake from you. Remember, Berners are stoic and will suffer in silence rather than displease their owners.

If your situation permits, the best of all worlds is to set up a dog run outside and let the pup sleep in it in good weather. It has to be below freezing for a puppy to be too cool. These are mountain dogs and love the cold. Provide the puppy with a few toys and an insulated dog house raised off the ground. In the summer provide the run with some form of shade for use during daylight. As much as possible, the puppy should be in the house with you so he will bond to you and your family. Introduce him to all your visitors so he will learn to meet and greet friendly callers properly. If you have very little company, he may become more protective than you want.

PUPPY PROBLEMS

There are probably more problems that can arise with the care of a new puppy than could possibly be covered in just one book. So this section will concentrate on those that appear most prevalent with puppy buyers in my experience.

Biting

The most prevalent difficulty seems to be aggression or puppy biting. Some owners have gone so far as to consult a dog psychologist to deal with what is normal puppy behavior. Puppies will bite or chew on almost everything with which they come into contact, including fingers. They are exploring the feel of everything and how it responds to them. The mistake most new owners make is allowing the puppy to chew on their hands and fingers as long as they do not bite down too hard. This encourages chewing that becomes harder and more assertive as the puppy grows. Chewing and biting must be discouraged from the onset. Any mouthing at all on any part of the human anatomy should be met with a loud "Oouuchh!" Remove the part from the puppys' mouth and refuse to continue any play, cuddling, holding or other positive interaction until this offensive behavior stops. Some puppies get the idea right away, others find this behavior to be worth the risk of your disapproval and refuse to give it up. You must be diligent in your disapproving responses and it will end, but some puppies are quite stubborn and take considerable convincing.

Children must be taught to never throw their hands up in the air and scream and run as this excites the puppy. He thinks this is some wonderful new game to play and will chase. Behavior such as this in children can turn a little biting problem into real aggression in play. Teach children to simply leave the puppy alone when it begins to bite and ignore it until it behaves properly.

Diarrhea

There can be many reasons for a pup to develop diarrhea. The stress of leaving the litter and going to new surroundings can cause a short bout. Stress can often cause a dormant protozoan infection in the intestinal tract, called coccidiosis, to become extremely active. Coccidiosis takes the form of diarrhea, often containing blood and mucus. The best way to diagnose it is through a stool sample evaluated by your veterinarian. The condition responds to several different drugs, the one most frequently prescribed is Albon. Often the entire litter is infected but only the pups stressed by long trips or shipping may ever show symptoms.

Worms

Roundworm Roundworms are extremely common parasites in puppies. Larvae of these worms often encyst in the muscles of the dam, and are activated during pregnancy, entering the puppy's blood-

246

stream through the placenta and causing a prenatal infestation. This makes it almost impossible to raise a worm-free litter, even with frequent worming. Symptoms are pot belly, thinness along the back-bone, poor coat condition, diarrhea and, in severe cases, the worms may be seen in the stool or vomited up. If roundworms are the only parasites present, a treatment or two with piperazine citrate should do the trick. Consult your veterinarian for dosage amounts and frequency.

Hookworm This parasite, like the roundworm, inhabits the small intestine, but is much more dangerous to the puppy. These worms can also be passed on as prenatal infestations, and their presence is characterized by diarrhea and anemia. This worm ingests blood, and a massive infestation can cause circulatory collapse, shock and death.

Tapeworm The tapeworm is different from other internal parasites. It requires an intermediate host to complete its life cycle. Its interme-diate host in connection with the dog is the flea, making its occur-rence quite common. Tapeworms are difficult to diagnose with a microscopic examination, as their eggs are in their body segments. These body segments appear in feces as "ricelike" pieces or some-times seen hanging from the anal area. If you observe these, inform your veterinarian so treatment may be prescribed.

Whipworm These are hard to find. Your vet may simply treat for whipworm if symptoms warrant. A puppy with whipworm is un-thrifty (does not gain weight), has bouts of diarrhea and vomiting and is often anemic.

Heartworm This parasite, like tapeworm, is also carried by an intermediate host, in this case the mosquito. It is transmitted from infected dogs by a mosquito that ingests blood filled with heartworm microfilaria. In the mosquito, the microfilaria develop into infective larvae. When the mosquito bites a healthy dog that dog becomes infected as well. After a period of development through several stages in the dog's muscles, the worms migrate to the heart and begin producing microfilaria, completing the cycle. Adult heartworms can be up to a foot in length. As adults they inhabit the heart muscle and pulmonary arteries. Prevention is the best answer. Check with your veterinarian and start your pup on a prevention program as soon as you get him home if this coincides with mosquito season. A dog afflicted with heartworm tires easily, coughs, has difficulty breathing and may even show signs of congestive heart failure. Sometimes a dog can be infected by male worms that will not produce microfilaria, thus not showing up on common tests. Treatment is possible, but it is long and severe. Stick with the "an ounce of prevention is worth a pound of cure" theory on this one.

Hot Spots

Hot spots are bacterial skin infections that begin as small, sticky spots and often appear to be wet. These spots progress rapidly into large swollen areas that often ooze yellowish-green pus. Treatment can be as simple as clipping away a little hair with scissors and treating with a little topical spray to shaving the entire area and treating with antibiotics as well as topical applications.

The condition is often caused by prolonged periods of exposure to wet weather or insufficient drying after bathing. Hot spots were once thought to be caused by a lack of adequate grooming, but this theory is questionable at best. I have found them to be the result of a combination of factors, but poor grooming can play a part, particularly in puppies. When puppies shed their undercoats acquired through a cold winter, all undercoat must be removed as soon as it loosens or hot spots can result.

These spots can be aggravated by the dog chewing and licking them, opening them up to outside infection. If left untreated they can become infected and can even be life-threatening. Further detection is in order by your veterinarian to diagnose an underlying cause, such as allergies or thyroid problems.

Bladder Infections

Bladder infections are quite common in female puppies. They are particularly prevalent in individuals who squat so low while urinating that the outer genitalia actually touches the ground. Mild cases often respond well to doses of 1500 mg. of vitamin C, twice a day. Symptoms are frequency of urination and inability to hold urine in puppies over four months of age.

Osteochondritis Dissecans (OCD)

Found in both the hip and shoulder joint, this condition is the result of trauma. The femoral or humoral head develops a lesion, or sometimes a small piece of cartilage or bone actually breaks off, floating free in the joint area and causing pain. It is believed that this may occur more often in large breeds because of the lack of blood supply to the joint. The symptoms are lameness, particularly in the forelimbs. It can come and go and often improves with rest only to show up again with exercise. It is not known if this condition is inherited. A predisposition may be inherited but this is only conjecture. Treatment is usually rest, but sometimes surgery is required. The best treatment is to try to avoid the possible causes; obesity, food too high in nutrients causing excessive early growth, open unsupervised play with older or larger dogs and exercising under hazardous conditions.

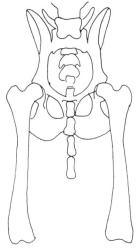

These hips, correctly positioned for X-ray evaluation, have received a rating of "Good" from the Orthopedic Foundation for Animals (OFA).

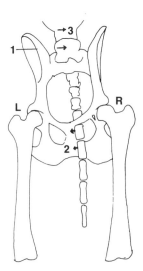

The same hips shown in the previous drawing, but with the pelvis rotated. Such rotation may show misalignment. The dog's left side was closer to the film from which this drawing was made, shown by the uneven appearance of the ilial wings (1). The left wing shows a much wider oval than the right wing; normally, both wings should match. Displacement of the pelvic symphysis to the left (2) and of the lumbar dorsal spinous process to the right of the midline (3) are indicated by the arrows. The right hip appears more shallow than the left hip compared to the well-positioned view in the previous drawing.

250

10

Nutrition and Common Health Problems

NUTRITION

The health of a Bernese Mountain Dog seems to be greatly influenced by the amount and type of food an individual dog is fed. It has been my experience that thinner dogs live longer, are less frequently afflicted by hip dysplasia and other physical problems. They also mature more slowly and are not as impressive as puppies as their heavier siblings. Thus there is a great tendency in this breed to overfeed. Sadly, many breeders and buyers alike select show puppies on the basis of weight alone. Obviously this is a great mistake, but in the absence of structural knowledge breeders and buyers alike fall back on bone (weight) and coat as the only qualifications needed to be a true Bernese. This misconception often sets up a lifelong pattern of overfeeding, and one sees very few old, obese dogs. A study in structure would help to end this practice.

Additionally, relying on the genetic makeup is a much more reliable way to select for size and substance. A small female bred to an extremely large male will not assure size and substance, as a sound small female bred to a large unsound male will also not assure soundness. Both parents must exhibit the qualities desired. Exceeding nutrition requirements only causes overly rapid growth in young dogs, which leads to skeletal problems and more. It will not make a dog whose genes dictate moderate size achieve any greater size than genetic coding will allow.

The type of food a dog is fed is also very important, particularly in a breed that is often afflicted with immune deficiency problems. Natural foods free of chemical preservatives fed in limited quantities maintains a healthy, long-lived dog. The following is a diet that I have found works extremely well:

Breakfast—2 cups Natural Life Condition Food dry, mixed with equal parts of Natural Life Lamaderm, one 500 mg. vitamin C tablet, one 400 mg. vitamin E tablet and 30–50 mg. zinc, moistened with warm tap water.

Dinner—2 cups of the Natural Life mix without the vitamins, moistened with warm tap water. Add 1 scoop of Nu-Pro when growing new coat.

My reasoning for this diet is that dogs stay healthy, keep the proper weight, maintain excellent muscle tone and flexibility and are rarely afflicted with hot spots or fleas. Should they go off their food, I try two or three tablespoons of canned food as a mixer and to stimulate an appetite. As soon as the dogs are eating normally again, I discontinue the canned. They are always fed limited quantities and four cups is a sufficient maintenance ration for most Bernese. Leaving food out at all times makes a dog a picky eater or leads to overweight, and draws mice and other vermin. Controlled-portion feeding is the way to go, and dividing the food into two meals a day will hopefully keep your dog safe from bloating.

COMMON HEALTH PROBLEMS

Cancer

I feel this is an important area for discussion. The Bernese Mountain dog is a dearly loved breed; I know of no other breed that can endear itself to its owner as this one. Therefore, the passing of one of these animals is devastating, and much study has been undertaken by the members of the Bernese Mountain Dog Club of America to try to extend the lives of these dogs. Along with these efforts has come considerable publicity to veterinarians, most of which is very good. But many veterinarians still surmise that if there is smoke, there must be fire, and so assume the worst when treating a Bernese. So let me dispel a few myths. First of all, Bernese do not have a corner on cancer cases. Histiocytosis, often referred to as "Bernese cancer" also occurs in other breeds. Bernese are also not the only breed that can die young of cancer—there are many others. There is a higher instance in Bernese, but it is not a plague. Not every bump and lump appearing on a Berner's body is a cancerous growth. Not every illness will result in death and not all Bernese have autoimmune problems. To scientifically study this cancer in Bernese, a controlled environment would have to be set up to rule out environmental influences. Affected dogs or offspring of affected dogs would have to be bred in a colony in an attempt to reproduce cancer in offspring. I don't believe anyone is ready to do that yet.

Sebaceous Cysts

Bernese live in unison with sebaceous gland tumors (or sebaceous cysts), which are common in all dogs. These cysts are epithelial growths arising from sebaceous gland cells, the cause of which is unknown, and clinical management is often observation without treatment. They may also be surgically removed, but often return in either the same place or a new location.

Water on the Elbow

This is often spontaneous, thought to be the result of flopping down hard on the elbows. Many veterinarians will drain these areas repeatedly, or install drains. This will often lead to hardening. The best treatment is to cushion the dog's sleeping area and make sure she sleeps there in a crate or by some other restraint, and allow these fluid-filled areas to reabsorb on their own.

Liver Shunts (Portal Vascular Anomalies)

This condition is often hard to detect if the affected dog is also a poor doer in general. She doesn't gain weight and is stunted in growth. Other symptoms are bizarre behavioral changes such as irrational hysteria or unpredictable aggression. Since Bernese are stoic, the symptoms may be as subtle as breaking housetraining without apparent reason.

Thyroid Function

This function has become the area most readily blamed for all problems, but without much scientific backup. First, normal T3 and T4 levels tend to be lower in large and giant breeds and old dogs, and higher in small breeds and very young dogs. T3 and T4 levels also show a rhythm, with a peak around noon. In addition, one study showed low basal serum T3 and T4 levels in 20 percent of 100 normal dogs, and normal basal levels in 30 percent of 250 hypothyroid dogs, and another study found normal basal serum T4 levels in over 50 percent of 60 hypothyroid dogs.

The current practice is to perform one simple T3, T4 test and if the result is normal, we assume the dog is normal. For abnormal readings we assume the foregoing rule of thumb to be true also. But in light of the prior information, you can see that is not the case. This has become a catchall area for poor coat, reproductive problems and a host of other situations.

I once picked a dog up from a handler (who has since retired), and in my rush to find a lead, knocked over a wash basin full of thyroid pills. There must have been forty bottles in it. When I looked very surprised, the handler informed me that every dog he showed was on thyroid. Can so many dogs be affected, or do we automatically throw every dog with an average coat on thyroid medication to grow coat and every bitch that doesn't conceive on thyroid medication to resolve her problems?

It seems strange that an area that is so poorly diagnosed could become the root of so many problems. Thyroid function needs much more research. Normal levels for individual breeds need to be established and scientifically tested to prove their accuracy. A test will hopefully be developed that can also determine with greater dependability the very existence of this problem. Don't be led astray by theory; dig deeper for scientific fact. If and when you attend a lecture on this problem, ask about control groups. Theories are not facts until they are put to the test. Don't be concerned if your dog tests on the low side of normal in a morning reading. Retest around noon and you may find your Bernese registering on the high side of normal.

Canine Hip Dysplasia

All dogs are susceptible to canine hip dysplasia, however large breeds are considered to have a higher incidence. The Bernese ranked number eight in CHD with 2,491 dogs evaluated by the Orthopedic Foundation for Animals from January 1974 to 1992. Of this number 25.5 percent were found to be dysplastic. This probably represents a much lower number than the actual population at large since most X-rays are taken in response to a clinical problem in the pet population and are not submitted to OFA. Another large segment of affected individuals are X-rayed simply for breeding credentials and are not submitted if the X-raying veterinarian determines that these dogs will not pass OFA standards. Again, since Bernese are ranked high in incidence, every little growth gimp is often blamed on CHD, and X-raying is done at very early ages. Let me once again dispel the myth that this breed is so prone to hip dysplasia. Consider that the Golden Retriever, not a particularly large dog and one of America's most popular pets, ranks number twelve with 44,025 evaluations and 23.5 percent affected—only 2 percent lower than the Bernese (based on OFA evaluations from January 1974 to July 1992). So yes, Bernese do have a rather high incidence of CHD, but it's not as bad as in some other breeds.

So you buy a pet and it ends up with CHD—it happens. No breeder can guarantee clear hips in puppies, only in parents. Responsible breeders do their best to produce good hips but they cannot play God. Hips are not directly inherited from the parents only. It is much like a blue-eyed inheritance pattern. It can show up even with unaffected parents, but it is less likely. Studies show unaffected parents can produce as much as 25 percent affected offspring. CHD is often not even detectable until a dog is quite old, or it can be very painful at a young age; however most mildly dysplastic dogs lead totally normal lives with no apparent problems. CHD is not a terminal condition as is occasionally supposed. Should your dog be diagnosed with CHD, and you are told she must have surgery in forty-eight hours or she will have to be euthanized, show another veterinarian your Berner's X-rays and get a second opinion.

What Do Good Hips Look Like? The femur heads are well seated (60 percent or more of the femoral head is covered by the acetabulum) in the acetabulum.

Are They Correctly Positioned? This was once thought to be unimportant by many breeders. If hips were dysplastic, no amount of positioning would help. Not true. Hips that are poorly positioned can appear to be dysplastic or fair instead of good. This is why many breeders ask to see the X-rays when a problem surfaces with a given dog's hips.

What Do the Ratings from OFA Means?

Excellent hip joint confirmation—A well-formed ''C''-shaped acetabulum and 75 percent or more of the femoral head covered by the acetabulum.

Good hip joint conformation—A well-formed ''C''-shaped acetabulum and 60 percent to 75 percent of the femoral head covered by the acetabulum.

Fair hip joint conformation—''Mild arthritis'' with mild irregularities or subluxation. Ossicles may be seen at the craniodorsal acetabular rim, but no evidence of joint laxity is seen.

Borderline hip joint conformation—conformation of the animal prevents determination or film-quality problems interfere with accurate interpretation (positioning, darkroom technique, exposure).

Mild CHD—Mild subluxation or shallow acetabulum with 40 percent to 50 percent of femoral head covered and minimal secondary changes.

Moderate CHD—Moderate subluxation with 25 percent to 40 percent of the femoral head covered or subluxation with evidence of secondary changes.

Severe CHD—Severe subluxation with less than 25 percent of the femoral head covered or moderate subluxation with marked secondary changes.

Elbow Dysplasia

Elbow dysplasia is not a dysplasia as the name suggests but rather a catchall term used to describe a group of degenerative joint diseases of the elbow: ununited anconeal process, fragmented medial coronoid process or osteochondritis of the medial humeral condyle. These diseases can only be diagnosed by radiograph. Normal elbows are only reported as normal by OFA, but abnormal elbows are rated by grades.

What Do the Grades Mean?

Grade 1—Minimal bone change on the anconeal process.

Grade 2—Additional subchondral bone changes and/or osteophytes.

Grade 3—Well-developed degenerative joint disease.

Elbow dysplasia can be caused by an injury, and the inheritance may be multiple. Once again breeders can only guarantee clear or normal elbows in the parents, not the offspring. Studies show even normal parents can produce as much as 34 percent affected progeny. Since elbow dysplasia is still relatively new to many breeders, some do not check parents. If a breeder finds a problem in a line with front lameness, he or she is often prompted to begin screening for elbow problems. Competitiveness with other breeders to prove their stock more worthy can also encourage some breeders to screen for such defects.

How Prevalent Is Elbow Dysplasia? As of this writing seventy breeds have been evaluated by OFA; twenty breeds were found to be affected. Breeds in which at least fifty affected individuals were found include the Bernese Mountain Dog. Bernese females were found to be 28.1 percent dysplastic (or 41 affected out of 146 submitted for evaluation), and 70.7 percent of these females were grade 1, 19.5 percent were grade 2 and 9.8 percent were grade 3. Bernese males were found to be 28.6 percent dysplastic (out of 91 submissions, 26 were affected), and 61.5 percent were grade 1, 26.9 percent were grade 2 and 11.5 percent were grade 3. With grade 1, only one elbow may be involved, but this is hard to determine. Other breeds were more or less affected with Rottweilers coming in at females 32.5 percent and males 44.6 percent dysplastic, so it could be worse. Many dogs with elbow dysplasia may never show any clinical signs, while others may have quite pronounced limps. Surgery can often be used to remove bone fragments and eliminate the limp.

How Can You Help? Your dog will either inherit a tendency toward dysplasia or she won't, but environment can play a role. Avoid the following:

- Rough play with older, heavier dogs.
- Climbing stairs frequently at a young age.
- Constant activity on slippery floors.
- Overnutrition, i.e., quantity. Feed controlled portions. The type of food (high protein or not) is not as important as the amount fed. Growth should be slow and steady with no excess weight. Do not try to get a mature look on a dog at an early age through feeding techniques.
- Open exercise on irregular terrain.
- Overexercising young dogs, using them as jogging companions or as part of other fitness regimens.
- In general, just use common sense.

Panosteitis

This is associated with large-boned, rapidly growing puppies. It is a painful inflammation of the bone marrow, expressed by a lameness that travels from one leg to another. "Pano" symptoms may appear in puppies as early as four months or as late as one year.

Eye Problems

Progressive Retinal Atrophy (PRA) Although seen extremely infrequently, a few cases of this eye problem have been diagnosed in Bernese Mountain Dogs. This is a form of "night blindness," that leads to total blindness and is hereditary.

Cataracts Again, this rarely occurs in Bernese but there have been a few cases. This can only be properly diagnosed by dilating the eyes. If you feel there is a problem, seek out a board-certified ophthalmologist in your area. A layman cannot properly examine for cataracts.

Entropion This condition is characterized by inverted eyelids, which force the eyelashes to brush against the cornea, causing constant weeping of the eyes and constant pain. If left unchecked, permanent damage to the eye may occur. This is a hereditary condition. Surgery will relieve the pain, but affected individuals should not be used for breeding. This condition occurs frequently in Bernese Mountain Dogs.

Ectropion This is a pout out of the lower lid in a turning-out formation, which exposes the conjunctiva in a pronounced manner. Although unsightly, this condition causes the dog no pain and does not require surgery except for cosmetic purposes.

Papillomas Cutaneous papillomas are common in dogs. Bernese tend to develop these in old age particularly in the tooth and gum areas, although they can also occur in other areas. They are cauliflowerlike growths, occurring more often in males than females, that are usually benign. Management can range from surgical removal to observation without treatment, unless they interfere with eating.